THE LIFE PORTRAITS OF
Thomas Jefferson

BY ALFRED L. BUSH

THOMAS JEFFERSON MEMORIAL FOUNDATION, INC.

CHARLOTTESVILLE, VIRGINIA

1987

Copyright © 1962 and 1987 by The Thomas Jefferson Memorial
Foundation, Inc.
Library of Congress Catalogue Card Number: 87-51205
ISBN Number: 0-8139-1163-x

THE PROFILE on the title page is based on the 1809 stipple engraving by David Edwin, which was engraved from a drawing by William Russell Birch, which was, in turn, drawn from the original of Gilbert Stuart's medallion profile of Jefferson. After Birch made his "correct drawing" of Stuart's medallion profile in October of 1805, he "thought of engraving it . . . but found [he] could not equal Mr. Edwin in it, got him to do it, took off a few impressions and sent [them to Jefferson], intending to rebite the plate to make it more lasting but spoilt the plate in attempt to rebite." These "few impressions," regarded by Jefferson as "an elegant specimen of Mr. Edwin's talent," bear the inscription "Jefferson. G. Stuart pinx W. Birch delin. D. Edwin sc. 1809 Copy Right secured according to law," and were engraved, according to Birch who assured Jefferson that his "purpose is to give them away," for "no other purpose then that a proper Likeness . . . may be circulated." When Jefferson presented one of them to his friend Horatio Gates Spafford in 1815, he described it as "a profile, engraved by Edwin from the original drawn by Stewart, and deemed the best which has been taken of me."

The Anthoensen Press, Portland, Maine

TO THE MEMORY OF
HOWARD CROSBY RICE, JR.

Discerning antiquarian
generous mentor
pre-eminent student of Jefferson in France

ACKNOWLEDGEMENTS
TO THE 1962 EDITION

JEFFERSON's willingness to share the Monticello collections was characteristic and invariable. Requests for the loan of paintings from artists who wished to copy them and publishers who hoped to reproduce them in prints were cordially granted by Jefferson, who was always eager to make his private collection available for the public's edification. The same willingness to share inestimable treasures characterizes the present owners of Jefferson's life portraits and has made this exhibition possible. To each of these individuals and institutions, as they are noted in these pages, goes the profound gratitude of the Board of Directors of The Thomas Jefferson Memorial Foundation for their generosity in lending the portraits in their possession, and my own thanks for the pleasant and helpful way in which all of them have facilitated the study of these portraits.

The idea of this exhibition and the enormous task of assembling the life portraits in Charlottesville is the work of James A. Bear, Jr., to whom I am grateful not only for the opportunity of compiling this catalogue but most especially for sharing with me his intimate knowledge of Jefferson's possessions.

It was the comprehensive gathering of documentation of all forms, under the direction of Julian P. Boyd as editor of *The Papers of Thomas Jefferson,* that brought together the iconographic materials that made possible the extensive study of Jefferson's portraits upon which this catalogue is based. I am further indebted to Mr. Boyd for his helpful criticism of the manuscript in its final stages.

Howard C. Rice, Jr., has generously and congenially allowed me to usurp his time whenever I ran into an iconographic problem, and his scholarly familiarity with Jefferson's portraits and Jefferson's France has enabled me to avoid a number of serious errors.

As must be most students of iconographic materials, I am deeply indebted to the Frick Art Reference Library, whose staff has saved me hours of searching by presenting me with likenesses that were discovered in the unending compilation of their inestimably useful files.

Of the other institutions and individuals who helped so generously in this ordering of Jefferson's portraits, I can mention here only those to whom I am most heavily indebted. Whitfield J. Bell, Jr., Anne F. Clapp, the late Courtney Campbell, Ulysse Desportes, Louisa Dresser, James W. Foster, Wendell D. Garrett, Gertrude D. Hess, Louis C. Jones, Sheldon Keck, Peter Michaels, Agnes Mongan, Elisabeth Packard, Anna Wells Rutledge, Caroline Scoon, Charles Coleman Sellers, Edward Suydam,

Olivia Taylor, David H. Wallace and H. Wade White have all been exceptionally generous in sharing their time and knowledge with me. In Princeton I have enjoyed not only the privilege of the pleasant and valuable consultation of Professors Donald Egbert and John Martin and of Gillett Griffin, but also the superb resources of the Marquand Library and the cooperation of its librarian, Frederica Oldach. While acknowledging the help of these many persons, I must also acknowledge that the responsibility for the statements and iconographic decisions made here is solely my own.

I am grateful also to the photographers who so excellently photographed the portraits for this catalogue. Paul P. Juley photographed the Edgehill Stuart, all three of the Peale portraits and those by Field, Polk, Savage, Valaperta and Cardelli. Stuart's medallion profile and the portrait by Mather Brown were photographed by George Cushing. Franklyn Rollins photographed Browere's plaster life mask.

It is a pleasure, also, to acknowledge the patience, congeniality, craftsmanship and valuable help of P. J. Conkwright and E. Harold Hugo, who have designed and produced this catalogue.

ACKNOWLEDGEMENTS
TO THE 1987 EDITION

OVER many years Howard C. Rice, Jr., faithfully brought pertinent materials to my attention, especially those issued in France, anticipating later editions of this catalogue.

William Howard Adams not only generated a new edition of this work in conjunction with his bicentennial Jefferson exhibition at the National Gallery of Art in 1976, but has also genially insisted that still another revision would be useful.

At Monticello, Daniel P. Jordan, Director of the Thomas Jefferson Memorial Foundation, has cleared the way for this new edition; while Susan R. Stein, its Curator, generously took the time to read through the revised text and offer valuable suggestions.

Robert A. Flynn of the Anthoensen Press nudged me toward the press and cheerfully accepted responsibility for what happened once the text was in his hands.

To these collaborators, and to many others whose assistance has not been so obvious, I offer thanks and appreciation.

THE LIFE PORTRAITS OF THOMAS JEFFERSON

The nine life portraits that are known, if at all, only through the subsequent reproduction of lost originals, are designated here by italics.

ARTIST	DATE	SURVIVING FORM	
1. *Mather Brown*	*1786*	*Replica in oils*	2
2. John Trumbull	1787 or 1788	Original in oils	6
3. *Edmé Quenedy*	*1789*	*Engraved copy in aquatint*	8
4. Jean-Antoine Houdon	1789	Original in marble	12
5. *Giuseppe Ceracchi*	*1791*	*Destroyed*	16
6. Charles Willson Peale	1791	Original in oils	18
7. *William Joseph Williams*	*1792*	*Not located*	
8. James Sharples	1797	Original in pastel crayon	24
9. *Tadeusz Kościuszko*	*1798*	*Engraved copy in aquatint*	28
10. Robert Field	ca. 1798	Original in watercolors	32
11. Charles Peale Polk	1799	Original in oils	34
12. Rembrandt Peale	1800	Original in oils	38
13. *Edward Savage*	*1800*	*Engraved copy in mezzotint*	42
14. *Gilbert Stuart*	*1800*	*Engraved copy in stipple*	46
15. A. B. Doolittle	1803	Original in verre églomisé	48
16. Fevret de Saint-Mémin	1804	Original in crayon	52
17. Rembrandt Peale	1805	Original in oils	54
18. Gilbert Stuart	1805	Original in oils	58
19. Gilbert Stuart	1805	Original in gouache	60
20. Bass Otis	1816	Original in oils	64
21. Giuseppe Valaperta	1816	Original in wax	68
22. *William John Coffee*	*1818*	*Not located*	
23. *Peter Cardelli*	*1819*	*Copy in plaster*	74
24. Thomas Sully	1821	Original in oils	76
25. John H. I. Browere	1825	Original in plaster	80

INTRODUCTION

THE discriminating and distinguished beholders who looked up from the misspelled catalogue entry under Houdon's name into the plaster visage of Jefferson in the late summer of 1789 in Paris viewed the American envoy's first portrait to be honored with public exhibition. It was an imposing debut: portrayed by the greatest portraitist of his time, surrounded by the landscapes of Hubert Robert and the classical allegories of David and scrutinized by an intelligent public, both sculptor and subject emerged from the honors of the Royal Salon to continue their pursuit of the elevated objectives implicit for both of them within this remarkable portrait.

Perhaps because their creations were received under less imposing circumstances and appreciated for less inherent reasons, Jefferson's subsequent portraitists in America were impelled to devote their talents to immortalizing "America's Distinguished Characters" in paint and pastel and plaster. A Gallery of American Worthies became the mandatory enterprise of the more ambitious of America's artists and the inclusion of a *Jefferson* imperative. And while these assemblies of the portraits of distinguished Americans too frequently reflected not so much the artist's recognition of his public responsibility as it did the promotion of his private interest, the imposing accomplishments of his subjects seldom allowed the portraitist to forget his obligation to history.

Appropriately, the task of creating Jefferson's final portrait fell to an artist who subordinated a desire for the public's immediate acclaim to an uncompromising regard for historical authenticity. It was Browere who recorded Jefferson's countenance for the last time before Jefferson "Bid adieu forever to busts and even portraits" and, within a year, to life itself. Ironically Browere's likeness began its public life by being unveiled on the very hour of Jefferson's death during the celebration of the semi-centennial of the Declaration of Independence. But as Jefferson and his portraitists passed into the realms of history, the full magnitude of their historic accomplishments was itself obscured. It was not, in fact, to be generally brought into focus until the commemoration of later anniversaries placed it at a proper distance and brought it pointedly to the public's attention. In the celebration of the Centennial of the Declaration of Independence and, most especially, the Centennial of the Inauguration of Washington, America's imagination was turned to its own past, and its eyes to the portraits of that past's most significant participants. In 1889 during the vast exhibition generated by the second of these centennials, Jefferson's portraits were gathered for the first time to receive the attention of the public and the exploratory study of scholars. Within a decade Charles Henry Hart made public the earliest ordering of the canon of Jefferson portraiture.

But it was an even later anniversary celebration—the bicentennial of Jefferson's birth—that was to focus attention on Jefferson's portraits at a time when his admirers included a scholar whose knowledge of Jefferson and ability in the analysis of iconographic materials enabled him to use that exhibition as the starting point for a study of such care and authority that all subsequent students of Jefferson's likenesses remain massively in his debt. It was the exceptional good fortune of Jefferson iconography to have had Fiske Kimball build from the elements set out by Charles Henry Hart, a foundation from which all further study could proceed solidly.

The bicentennial exhibition of 1943 at the National Gallery assembled fourteen portraits representing ten distinct likenesses of Jefferson. The 1962 exhibition sponsored by the Thomas Jefferson Memorial Foundation at the University of Virginia Museum of Fine Arts included twenty-four likenesses of Jefferson, representing twenty-four separate life likenesses. While the 1943 exhibition presented but four portrayals executed from life, the 1962 exhibition included fifteen life portraits. This revision of the catalogue of that exhibition retains all but one of those portraits—the pencil drawing thought in 1962 to have been drawn from life by Benjamin Latrobe. Both of those assertions are now in question. The twenty-five portraits enumerated here, of which only sixteen are known in their original form, comprise a canon of portrayals representing the work of twenty-three artists responsible for twenty-five distinct likenesses of Jefferson: twice the number of life portraits recorded by Kimball in his 1944 study.

Silhouettes have arbitrarily been eliminated from this work since the information on Jefferson's appearance that their outlines offer is so limited and because of the undocumented nature of the majority of them. Few are recorded as exactly as is that by Uri H. Hill who was introduced in June of 1803 to Jefferson by John Hawkins in a letter that furnishes the date, the method of execution and even a proposal for the work's future use. With the exception of these shadow portrayals, this catalogue represents every portrait of Jefferson now known to have been created from life.

On the following pages the essential information on each of Jefferson's life portraits is listed systematically with seven descriptive elements isolated to make reference and comparison convenient. The focus of the description in every instance is the life portrait, whether now extant or lost.

The dimensions of the portraits described here follow Stauffer in being expressed in inches and sixteenths of an inch. Thus 20.3 x 10.12 inches signifies 20 3/16 x 10 3/4 inches. When the original of the portraits reproduced on these pages is smaller than the format of this catalogue, it is reproduced at exact size.

The references noted at the end of the entry for each portrait cite only those sources that document the preceding statements and are most pertinent to the specific portrait. It should be assumed that the further sources for each artist listed in George C. Groce and David H. Wallace, *The New-York Historical Society's Dictionary of Artists in America* (New Haven, 1957), were also consulted and are frequently relied upon for the context of these entries. Another source of information on each of these likenesses, which I have not always cited but have invariably consulted and found useful, is the files of the Frick Art Reference Library. The prints that are noted individually here are identified, when possible, by their numerical designation in David M. Stauffer, *American Engravers Upon Copper and Steel* (New York, 1907). A few European prints are noted by their number in Stanislaus V. Henkels, *The* [Carson] . . . *Collection of Engraved Portraits of Thomas Jefferson* . . . (Philadelphia, n.d.). The following works are cited so frequently that short titles have been employed:

Adams: William Howard Adams (Ed.), *The Eye of Thomas Jefferson,* Washington, D.C., 1976, reprinted, Charlottesville, 1981.

Bowen: Clarence W. Bowen (Ed.), *The History of the Centennial Celebration of the Inauguration of George Washington,* New York, 1892.

Boyd: Julian P. Boyd (Ed.), *The Papers of Thomas Jefferson,* Princeton, 1950–.

Bush: "The Life Portraits of Thomas Jefferson," in *Jefferson and the Arts: An Extended View,* William Howard Adams (Ed.), Washington, D.C., 1976.

Cunningham: Noble E. Cunningham, Jr., *The Image of Thomas Jefferson in the Public Eye, Portraits for the People, 1800–1809,* Charlottesville, 1981.

Hart: Charles Henry Hart, "The Life Portraits of Thomas Jefferson," *McClure's Magazine,* Vol. XI, No. 1 (May 1898), 47–55.

Kimball: Fiske Kimball, "The Life Portraits of Jefferson and Their Replicas," *Proceedings of The American Philosophical Society,* Vol. LXXXVIII (1944), 497–534.

While every effort has been made to make this catalogue a definitive one, it is emphatically hoped that this claim will soon prove unwarranted, for few prospects are more pleasant to the student of Jefferson than the discovery of further portraits deserving a place among the company of Jefferson's life likenesses. One of the foremost objectives of this publication has been the stimulation of an informed interest in Jefferson's portraits that might make possible the recognition of further life likenesses as yet unidentified in public or private collections.

It is hoped that this gathering of Jefferson's portraits will suggest in a cumulative and memorable way what was the invariable objective of each of their creators: an authentic and penetrating portrayal of the man in whose presence each of these likenesses was created.

THE LIFE PORTRAITS OF
THOMAS JEFFERSON

1. The Adams replica of the lost life portrait of Jefferson painted in London in 1786 by Mather Brown. The collection of Mr. Charles Francis Adams, Dover, Massachusetts.

1. THE PORTRAIT BY MATHER BROWN

Unlocated

MEDIUM: John Adams's commission for a duplicate of this lost painting and Trumbull's difficulty in distinguishing correctly between the Adams replica and the life portrait indicate that not only in content, but also in medium, the original painting was duplicated in the extant replica: that it was an oil on canvas, measuring approximately 36 x 28 inches.

AUTHORSHIP: Presumably the life portrait bore an inscription identical to that still legible on the face of the Adams replica: "M Brown pt 1786." This inscription, the artist's receipt on the reverse of the replica, Jefferson's entry in his accounts for payment to Brown for the portrait, and the report in the *New-York Packet* of 19 October 1786 of the portrait's presence in Brown's studio are only four of many contemporary documents that indisputably establish Brown's authorship of this likeness. Trumbull doubted that the painting destined for Jefferson, which he saw in Brown's painting rooms in the spring of 1788, was the life portrait, but the artist's agreement "that the original should be" Jefferson's, and the difference in the size of payments made by Adams and Jefferson, indicate that the latter did receive the original canvas.

CHRONOLOGY: The missing life portrait was painted at Mather Brown's London studio in Cavendish Square sometime between Jefferson's arrival in London on 11 March 1786 and his departure on the 26th of the following month. The final sitting, in fact, may well have taken place the day before Jefferson set out for France when he made his payment of ten pounds to Brown for the painting. The portrait depicts Jefferson at 43 as America's Minister Plenipotentiary to the Court of Versailles, "the engaging and intelligent favorite of the Paris salons." Brown, though in his sixth year of painting in England and among the more fashionable of London's portraitists, was himself a young American of only 24 years of age.

HISTORY: Painted on Jefferson's commission, the portrait remained in Brown's studio for more than two years awaiting the completion of the portrait of Adams that was to accompany it. Trumbull saw the painting in the artist's rooms in the spring of 1788 and at Jefferson's request supervised its shipment to Paris late that summer. Carefully packed with other paintings purchased by Jefferson, it left London on the 16th of August 1788, and Jefferson acknowledged receiving the "pictures in good condition" on the 10th of September. Nothing of the portrait's subsequent history is known.

CONDITION: The life portrait is thought to have been destroyed in Jefferson's lifetime. Kimball suggested that it may have been part of the baggage that was looted and thrown into the James River when Jefferson retired from the presidency or that it was among the possessions that Jefferson had given to his granddaughter, Ellen Wayles Coolidge, which were subsequently lost at sea.

ICONOGRAPHIC IMPORTANCE: The opinion that Trumbull wrote Jefferson in March of 1788 after seeing Brown's portraits of both Adams and Jefferson ("Mr. Adams is like. Yours I do not think so well of.") was one that was apparently shared by a number of Jefferson's friends. William Short reported that while the "picture by Brown of Mr. Adams is an excellent likeness; that of Mr. Jefferson is supposed by every body here to be an étude. It has no feature like him." It was undoubtedly because of this inadequacy that Mather Brown's portrait came to play only a peripheral role in shaping the public image of Jefferson. Even in more recent times, with the original canvas lost and the replica in private hands, it has never been widely known. Apart from its failure as a characteristic portrayal of its subject, the portrait is admired now, as Short's description of it as an "étude" suggests it was in his time, as one of the most attractive of Brown's works. It is also the earliest of the identified portraits of Jefferson.

COPIES: The receipt pasted on the reverse of the replica commissioned by John Adams dates its completion to shortly before 12 May 1786. This is the portrait that Abigail Adams wrote Jefferson of the following month, as dignifying a part of the Adams's London residence, and which has descended through the Adams family to its present owner, Mr. Charles Francis Adams of Dover, Massachusetts. The portrait seems not to have been further reproduced until 1860 when Timothy House's engraving of it appeared as the frontispiece to George Bancroft's *History of the United States*. A later print, engraved for *Appleton's Cyclopaedia of American Biography* in 1887 by A. B. Hall, copied the Adams replica more faithfully.

REFERENCES: Bowen, 1892, 486; Hart, 1898, 49; Kimball, 1944, 499–501; Boyd 1:lvii, facing 3, 10:161, 11:169, 12:206, 358, 597, 647, 13:178, 199, 280, 345, 519, 597; William Kelby, *Notes on American Artists*, New York, 1922, 29; Massachusetts Historical Society *Proceedings*, Vol. 47 (1913), 32–4; Adams, 1976, 140, 141, 369, 394; Bush, 1976, 20–23.

2. THE PORTRAIT BY JOHN TRUMBULL

The Yale University Art Gallery

MEDIUM: Trumbull's life portrait of Jefferson is painted in oil directly onto the canvas of the artist's small *Declaration of Independence*, which measures 21.2 x 31.2 inches.

AUTHORSHIP: The importance and fame of the small canvas of the *Declaration of Independence* is such that Trumbull's authorship of it has been a matter of common knowledge not only to his but to subsequent generations. The existence of three miniature portraits of Jefferson by Trumbull, all obviously related to the *Declaration* likeness, however, has frequently led students to identify one of these miniatures as the life portrait from which the Jefferson in the *Declaration* canvas was painted. Even after the discovery of Trumbull's explicit statement that the life portrait was painted directly into the "original small Declaration of Independence," Kimball still could not "resist the conclusion that the Church miniature was painted in 1786, a year before the Declaration"—thus identifying it as another, and earlier, portrait from life. But the letter of 19 December 1788 from William Short to Trumbull, which notes that the Church and Cosway miniatures are "each . . . a copy of Mr. Jefferson's picture" and suggests the painting of still another replica for Martha Jefferson, establishes all three of these miniatures as replicas of the portrait painted "from the life" into the original *Declaration of Independence*.

CHRONOLOGY: Despite Trumbull's statement that he painted his portrait of Jefferson in "the autumn of 1787" while in Paris executing portraits of the French officers for his depiction of the surrender at Yorktown, it was not until late December of that year that Trumbull arrived in France. The portrait, portraying Jefferson at 44, was painted in Jefferson's Paris residence, the Hôtel de Langeac, sometime between Trumbull's arrival in Paris on 19 December 1787 and the 16th of February 1788 when the painter was once again en route for London. Trumbull had written Jefferson in August of 1787 that he supposed "winter the most certain time of meeting" in Paris the French officers whose portraits were to be painted into his *Surrender at Yorktown*. Thus in these two winter months Trumbull, at but 31 years of age, painted not only "Mr. Jefferson in the original small Declaration of Independence" but also "Major General Ross in the small sortie from Gibraltar, and the French officers in the Surrender of Lord Cornwallis, At Yorktown"—likenesses, "all painted from the life in Mr. Jefferson's house," which Trumbull regarded "as the best of [his] small portraits."

HISTORY: The painting left Trumbull's hands in 1832 when it became the possession of Yale College as a result of the indenture of 19 December 1831 in which Trumbull presented this and other paintings to the college in exchange for an annuity of one thousand dollars a year, on the condition that "the said paintings shall never be sold, alienated, divided or dispersed, but shall always be kept together, and exhibited." As part of the "largest and finest collection of the works of the chief recorder of the American

5

2. A detail of John Trumbull's original *Declaration of Independence* showing Jefferson painted from life during the winter of 1787–88 at Jefferson's Paris residence. The Yale University Art Gallery.

Revolution," this portrait was hung in the small neoclassical Trumbull Gallery, which opened to the public on the Yale campus on 25 October 1832. The collection was moved in 1868 to Street Hall and again in 1928 to its present quarters in the Yale University Art Gallery.

CONDITION: In the perpetual care of the curatorial staff at Yale, the painting has been preserved in excellent condition.

ICONOGRAPHIC IMPORTANCE: Not only did Trumbull hold this portrait as among "the best of [his] small portraits," but Sizer captioned it unreservedly as the "painter at his best." Working with an eye to historical fidelity, Trumbull, representing Jefferson with unpowdered hair, in the costume of the earlier decade, and towering above his associates, has given us an image of Jefferson that undoubtedly comes remarkably close to depicting him as he appeared at the time of the presentation of his great literary achievement. This conception of the presentation of the Declaration of Independence has come to be the preeminent icon not only of the birth of the nation but also of Jefferson's imposing position in the early events of the Revolution.

COPIES: The two miniatures painted from the life portrait for Maria Cosway, who asked Jefferson just after Trumbull's return to London early in March to give the painter "leave to make a Coppy" of the portrait, and Angelica Schuyler Church (now, respectively, at the White House and the Metropolitan Museum of Art) were in their hands by July of 1788. The following September William Short, knowing of these two replicas, suggested that Trumbull "do a very clever gallant thing": "*Send a copy of the same to Miss Jefferson.*" This replica, modified considerably, was received by Jefferson's daughter in Paris in the last days of 1788 and is now at Monticello. Trumbull also painted replicas of the *Declaration,* and thus of Jefferson, twice. The first, with the figures the size of life, was painted in 1818 and is now in the rotunda of the Capitol at Washington. The second, painted in 1832 with figures at half life size, is owned by the Wadsworth Atheneum. The earliest of the numerous prints of the *Declaration* was engraved by Asher B. Durand in 1823.

REFERENCES: Bowen, 1892, 486; Hart, 1898, 47; Kimball, 1944, 501–5; Theodore Sizer, *The Works of Colonel John Trumbull,* New Haven, 1950, 35, 72–3, plate 13; Theodore Sizer (Ed.), *The Autobiography of John Trumbull,* New Haven, 1953, 152, 285–8; Elizabeth Cometti, "Maria Cosway's Rediscovered Miniature of Jefferson," *William and Mary Quarterly,* 3d ser., IX (1952), 152–5; Boyd 10:xxix–xxx, 12:358, 405, 603, 645, 14:364–5, 440; Adams, 1976, 101–103, 196, 379, 399; Bush, 1976, 23–26.

3. The aquatint profile of Jefferson engraved about 1801 by Edmé Quenedy from the print engraved in 1789 by Gilles-Louis Chrétien or from this print's ultimate source: the now lost physiognotrace portrait drawn from life by Edmé Quenedy in crayon on paper on the 23rd of April 1789 in Paris. The Yale University Art Gallery.

3. THE PORTRAIT BY EDMÉ QUENEDY

Unlocated

MEDIUM: Quenedy's original life-sized portrait of 1789 was undoubtedly drawn in crayon on paper, as are the few surviving examples of his original physiognotrace delineations. The portrait was begun with the tracing, by means of the physiognotrace, of Jefferson's profile. Into this outline the details of the subject's features were then drawn by the artist. Unlike Saint-Mémin, whose later physiognotrace drawings were sold as finished portraits along with the small engravings made from them, it seems that Quenedy regarded the large drawings only as a preliminary step to the final product: the engraved miniature profiles printed from the copper plate onto which Quenedy's partner, Gilles-Louis Chrétien, transferred the original drawing by means of a pantograph.

AUTHORSHIP: The only surviving version of this likeness is the print engraved from it about 1801. The inscription on the one example of this aquatint that survives with a legend indicates that the original was drawn from life by Edmé Quenedy. This identification is confirmed by the inscriptions on the engravings produced in 1789 by the Quenedy-Chrétien partnership, which invariably read (in abbreviated form): "Dessiné par Quenedy, gravé par Chrétien inventeur du physionotrace."

CHRONOLOGY: Jefferson's account book, Gouverneur Morris's diary and Quenedy's record of ticket holders all show that Jefferson sat for the portrait in Paris at the Quenedy-Chrétien establishment in the Rue Croix des Petits Champs just east of the Palais Royal on the 23rd of April 1789. Six days later Jefferson called for the copper plate upon which Chrétien had engraved Quenedy's delineation, and twelve prints struck from it.

HISTORY: While Jefferson purchased a dozen engravings and the plate from which they were taken, the original drawing apparently remained in the artist's hands, although it is uncertain whether it was purposely preserved by him. It has been plausibly suggested that the drawing may still have been in the artist's possession at the time of Jefferson's election to the presidency and that it was from this that Quenedy then re-engraved the portrait, perhaps with the intention of commercial distribution. It is also possible that this version of the portrait may have been engraved by Quenedy not from the original drawing but from a proof, retained for the artist's collection, of the 1789 Chrétien engraving of the likeness. Not only does there seem to be no record of the large original drawing, other than its delineation, but even more surprisingly, nothing is known of the history of the small copper plate or of the twelve examples of the 1789 engraving other than their purchase by Jefferson from the artist.

CONDITION: Since none of Quenedy's large physiognotrace drawings are extant, and since he apparently considered them merely a preliminary step in the execution of the engraved miniatures, it seems unlikely that his crayon original of Jefferson has survived.

9

ICONOGRAPHIC IMPORTANCE: The fact that examples of the engravings of this portrait are not mentioned as enclosures in any of Jefferson's letters to friends in America in the months immediately after their execution and that none are known to survive among the effects of Jefferson's friends in France suggests that Jefferson was more interested in the mechanical aspects of the physiognotrace than he was pleased with the likeness that resulted from his first contact with it. It is as what is very probably the first portrait of an American taken by means of this invention and one that records with exactness the outline of Jefferson's profile that this portrait deserves our attention, rather than as a portrayal of insight. Since even the engravings struck about 1801 survive in such rare instances, the portrait, doubtless, had but a limited circulation.

COPIES: Neither the copper plate, engraved by Chrétien, nor any of the twelve prints (almost certainly showing the profile against a circular background) that Jefferson purchased has ever been found. Only three examples of the aquatint, engraved by Quenedy most probably about 1801 (depicting the profile against an irregular oval background), have been located. The Bibliothèque Nationale possesses one with, and one without, an inscription; another example of the latter, a proof before letters, is owned by the Yale University Art Gallery.

REFERENCES: Kimball, 1944, 497; René Hennequin, *Les Portraits au Physionotrace*, Troyes, 1932, 59–60; Howard C. Rice, Jr., "A 'New' Likeness of Thomas Jefferson," *William and Mary Quarterly*, 3d ser., VI, No. 1 (Jan. 1949), [84]–9; Boyd 14:xlii–xliv, facing 361; Adams, 1976, 147, 370, 398; Bush, 1976, 26–29.

4. THE PORTRAIT BY JEAN-ANTOINE HOUDON

The Museum of Fine Arts, Boston

MEDIUM: Cut from Saravezza marble, the bust measures 21.4 inches high.

AUTHORSHIP: The marble is inscribed under the left shoulder "houdon f 1789." The fame of Houdon's likeness, the signatures on the original examples of it, and the unrivaled competence of its sculptor eliminate any doubt as to its authorship. Since there is no record of a terra cotta of this bust, the original clay maquette modeled by Houdon from life was most probably discarded in the process of making the mold from which at least three plaster examples were cast and finished by Houdon. Two of these, the Williamson example at the New-York Historical Society and the Rittenhouse example at the American Philosophical Society—both publically exhibited for more than a century in their respective institutions—are unquestionably from the hand of Houdon himself and are direct casts from the mold of the original portrait. But a plaster bust was regarded by the sculptor as only a temporary and intermediary stage in the production of a final portrait in some permanent substance such as bronze or marble. Fortunately this final form of Houdon's *Jefferson,* which Giacometti assumed must have been executed, though it was not documented as having been begun or completed and no such marble had surfaced by 1927, came to light about the time of the publication of Giacometti's authoritative study of Houdon's works. Because of the emergence of this marble from obscurity "at just the same period" that there appeared on the art market a number of other Houdon portraits of American subjects, "some with signatures or dates obviously erroneous, and some of them under circumstances very difficult to explain," and because "sculptors" considered it uncharacteristic of the work of Houdon's studio, Kimball questioned the genuineness of this marble. Statements of its authenticity by both Giacometti and Souffrice, the identification of the stone as Saravezza marble (that preferred and most used by Houdon), laboratory evidence that the bust is indeed an old one, the positive results of a comparison of this marble with other busts indisputably from Houdon's studio, and an unbroken and verifiable provenance tracing it, if not to Houdon's studio, into hands contemporary with it, seem, however, abundant justification to give this marble a place among the life portraits.

CHRONOLOGY: On 3 July 1789 Jefferson not only acknowledged the receipt of portrait busts from Houdon but also recorded the payment of 1000 livres to the sculptor for these busts. The purchase included, besides the portraits of other worthies, one, and perhaps two or three, examples of the *Jefferson.* By the end of the following month another plaster of the bust was on public exhibition at the Salon in 1789. These circumstances indicate that the clay likeness had been completed by the middle of that year, but it can only be assumed that the marble portrait was actually executed not long before Jefferson's purchase of the plaster examples of it. Although the inscribed date on the

11

4. The marble bust of Jefferson sculpted in Houdon's studio from an intermediary plaster example of the portrait modeled from life by Jean-Antoine Houdon sometime before July of 1789 in Paris. The Museum of Fine Arts, Boston.

marble could record only the year of the sitting and not necessarily that of the execution, it suggests that it was completed sometime between the Salon of 1789 and the end of the year.

HISTORY: The absence of any record of a payment for the marble in Jefferson's accounts indicates that the tradition that the marble was originally a gift from Jefferson to Destutt de Tracy is not correct. But as Kimball pointed out, after the summer Salon in which the plaster *Jefferson* was exhibited, de Tracy or any of Jefferson's French admirers could have had a marble executed at any time from Houdon's studio. It is recorded that the Boston marble was owned by the comtesse Sarah de Destutt, the daughter-in-law of Jefferson's admirer, and that it passed in 1839 into the possession of the related family of Leclercq de Chateauvieux at Melun. A civil paper of 1868 records that the bust was inherited by Ferdinand Leclercq who sold it in 1928. The bust thereafter passed into the hands of the Marie Sterner Gallery in New York, from which it was purchased in 1934 by the Museum of Fine Arts, Boston.

CONDITION: Excepting some few chips broken from the clothing at the front base of the bust, the marble is in superb condition. Its sharply cut lines suggest the full power of Houdon's portrait in a way in which the plasters, by the nature of the medium, cannot.

ICONOGRAPHIC IMPORTANCE: This superb likeness of Jefferson, by the greatest portraitist of his time, has been almost constantly displayed in its many versions in public and private collections since its original exhibition in the Salon of 1789. The high quality of the portrait and its extensive and enduring influence in shaping the public image of Jefferson has suggested, perhaps more than has any other likeness, a visual image that adequately encompasses the full range of his accomplishment and the elevated nature of his objectives.

COPIES: At least four examples of the bust may date to the year of its execution. Besides the Boston marble and the plasters at the New-York Historical Society and the American Philosophical Society, the Boilly paintings of Houdon at work record that a bust of Jefferson was still in Houdon's studio as late as 1804, although nothing is known of the subsequent history of the latter nor of any examples of the Houdon kept by Jefferson himself. Two other examples came to light when, in 1963, the French Fine Arts Administration provided an export permit for a plaster acquired by Roy Chalk of Washington, D.C., but only after another was donated to the French government by Edmond Courty. The latter bust is now in the collections of the Musée de Blérancourt. Copies in *biscuit de Sèvres* were reproduced commercially by the Manufacture de Sèvres during Houdon's lifetime, and later the bust was copied in America in various media. An engraving by Longacre of the bust was used as the frontispiece of Tucker's 1837 biography of Jefferson. The presidential portrait on the Indian Peace medal of 1801 by John Reich was, as Jefferson himself reported, "taken from Houdon's bust." A century after examples of this medal were given by Lewis and Clark to many of the Indians met in the course of their expedition, the Reich medal was used as the basis of the obverse of the Jefferson dollar, minted in 1903 to commemorate the centennial of the Louisiana Pur-

13

chase. Thirty-five years later another medallist, Felix Schlag, also chose the Houdon for the representation of Jefferson in the first design of a United States coin to be selected in open competition: the Jefferson nickel. Since its first issue in 1938, this version of Houdon's portrait has undoubtedly become the most widely circulated of all Jefferson likenesses.

REFERENCES: Bowen, 1892, 489; Hart, 1898, 50; Kimball, 1944, 505–7; Gilbert Chinard (Ed.), *Houdon in America*, Washington, 1930; G. Giacometti, *La Vie et l'œuvre de Houdon*, Paris, 1929; "Portrait Sculpture by Houdon," *Bulletin of the Museum of Fine Arts*, Vol. XXXII, No. 193 (Oct. 1934), 70–4; Thomas Jefferson to Martha Jefferson Randolph, 2 April 1802 in the Jefferson Papers at the Massachusetts Historical Society; correspondence with Mrs. Robin Esch at the Museum of Fine Arts, Boston; R. S. Yeoman, *A Guide Book of United States Coins*, Racine, 1950, 88–9, 184; Max Terrier, "Le Buste de Thomas Jefferson par Houdon," *Les Amis du Musée de Blérancourt*, 1965, 6–8; Brooke Hindle, *David Rittenhouse*, Princeton, 1964, 336; Adams, 1976, 136; Bush, 1976, 29–33.

5. THE PORTRAIT BY GIUSEPPE CERACCHI

Destroyed

MEDIUM: The marble bust, larger than life and "representing Mr. Jefferson in the Roman costume," which Ceracchi considered the finished form of this portrait, was cut in his studio in Florence from the terra cotta model that he had modeled from life. If the bust were characteristic of Ceracchi's work in America, it was admired not only as a faithful and lively likeness but also for its archaeological look as a "romanized" portrait produced in the full maturity of the artist's work.

AUTHORSHIP: That Ceracchi was the author of the colossal bust that stood in Jefferson's lifetime in the Hall at Monticello and was destroyed in the 1851 Library of Congress fire has never been doubted. The surviving correspondence between the artist and Jefferson concerning the disposition of the marble and the fame of the bust during the half century of its existence abundantly confirm the correctness of this identification. Since the destruction of the original marble, however, various busts have been erroneously labeled as copies of the destroyed original. Perhaps the earliest of these mistaken identifications is that of Lipscomb and Bergh who, in their 1903 edition of Jefferson's writings, captioned the mid-nineteenth-century bust by Henry Dmochowski Saunders as by "Ciracchi." In 1944 Kimball, misled by the vagueness of its provenance, identified the plaster bust then at Monticello as a copy of Ceracchi's marble. But this bust is now known to have been "made in the same mould in which was cast the fine, life-size, bronze statue . . . [by] the celebrated David [d'Angers]."

CHRONOLOGY: Jefferson received Ceracchi for the first time on the 2nd of March 1791 in Philadelphia when the sculptor was almost forty years of age. The terra cotta was modeled sometime shortly after that date, most probably before Jefferson left for New England in May. It is likely that Jefferson sat for Ceracchi in the sculptor's rooms in Mrs. Mary House's famous boarding establishment at Fifth and Market Streets—just a block north of the State House—where Madison also had rooms that year and where Jefferson himself had lived briefly in 1782–3. Among the most celebrated European sculptors of the day, Ceracchi had some twenty years of professional work as a distinguished portraitist behind him when he portrayed Jefferson, who was then 48.

HISTORY: The terra cotta maquette of the Jefferson, along with other preliminary matter for Ceracchi's proposed monument to the American Revolution, was shipped to Leghorn, Italy, where it was claimed by the sculptor early in 1793. As soon as the terra cotta was in his hands, Ceracchi announced that he would set to work on the colossal marble, which, he led Jefferson to believe, he was to present to him as a gift. The marble bust arrived at Monticello in the spring of 1795 when Ceracchi himself was again in America, but the "gift," which Jefferson had reluctantly accepted as a mark of Ceracchi's "flattering" esteem, was soon followed by the sculptor's bill for "one thousand five hundred Dollars." Despite the embarrassment of this deception and the fact that a final

15

5. A pencil sketch of the destroyed colossal marble bust of Jefferson by Giuseppe Ceracchi, which was sculpted from a terra cotta (now lost) modeled from life in Philadelphia not long after 2 March 1791. Ceracchi's portrait is depicted in this sketch supported by a broken column and ornamented pedestal, which was presented to Jefferson as such a genuine and generous "remembrance of . . . friendship" that it contrasts ironically with the nature of Ceracchi's "gift" that surmounts it. On an August evening in 1789 Jefferson returned to his Paris residence from Versailles to discover "a magnificent pedestal erected" in the hall in his absence. It was the gift of Madame de Tessé that came eventually to stand in the Hall at Monticello as the base of Ceracchi's colossal marble. After Jefferson's death, in fact, it accompanied that bust to its place in the Library of Congress where the ensemble was described in 1834 as "a splendid work; the bust is elevated upon the frustum of a fluted black marble column, based upon a circular pedestal, which is ornamented at the top by a continuous series of cherubs' heads, under a broad band encircling the pedestal, on which is sculptured the twelve signs of the zodiac. . . ." The pedestal bore an inscription, which Robert Mills translated to read: "To the Supreme Ruler of the Universe, under whose watchful care the liberties of N. America were finally achieved, and under whose tutelage the name of Thomas Jefferson will descend forever blessed to posterity." Like the portrait it supported, the pedestal was destroyed in the Library of Congress fire of 1851.

This sketch in light pencil was drawn on the reverse of Thomas Jefferson Randolph's retained copy of his letter to the Louisiana legislature dated 26 December 1826, in which he discusses the bust (now in the Edgehill-Randolph collection, the University of Virginia Library).

agreement on the payment to Ceracchi was not reached until 1800, Jefferson and his family admired the marble and gave it a conspicuous place in the Hall at Monticello where it was seen by William Wirt, who described it as "that exquisite and finished bust of the great patriot himself, from the master-hand of Caracci." Although it was "Jefferson's wish that his bust, executed by Ciracchi . . . would be presented" to the University of Virginia at his death, "the deeply embarrassed state in which his affairs were left" forced his executors to offer the bust for sale. When this was learned, many of the Charlottesville citizens present at the January 1827 sale of Jefferson's effects at Monticello petitioned the Virginia Assembly to purchase the bust as "the only sculptured memorial in Virginia of the Author of *The Declaration of Independence*," but their request was never acted upon. When Monticello was sold in 1831, the marble was removed to Edgehill, where it remained until purchased for the Library of Congress. There, in an honored place in the main reading room, it was destroyed in the fire of 1851.

CONDITION: Contemporary accounts of the Library of Congress fire leave no doubt that the bust was totally destroyed.

ICONOGRAPHIC IMPORTANCE: Considered by Jefferson as the *chef d'œuvre* of all the attempts at his portrait, regarded by his family as an "excellent likeness" of Jefferson in "the prime of life" and as a "grand and commanding object," called by William Thornton a "superb bust, one of the finest I have ever beheld," there is little doubt that the loss of this marble—presumably the earliest portrait of Jefferson executed in the United States and the first likeness of an American as secretary of state—leaves the most regrettable lacuna in Jefferson iconography.

COPIES: The terra cotta maquette—the original sculptured maquette modeled from life—was seen by Thomas Hubert, a Philadelphia merchant, in the studios of the Pisanni brothers in Florence not long before January of 1803. Its present location, despite extensive searches in Florentine collections, is unknown. William Thornton was given permission in 1816 by Jefferson to copy the Ceracchi in plaster, but apparently did not take advantage of the opportunity. Daguerreotypes known to have been taken by Robert Mills after Congress refused him permission to copy the bust in plaster in 1850 have not been located. The only delineation of the bust that is now known is the crude sketch, now at the Alderman Library of the University of Virginia, drawn on the verso of Thomas Jefferson Randolph's letter to the state of Louisiana, which was seeking to purchase it in 1826.

REFERENCES: Bowen, 1892, 489; Hart, 1898, 47; Kimball, 1944, 510–11; James A. Bear, Jr., "The Giuseppe Ceracchi Bust of Jefferson," an unpublished typescript; the Jefferson-Ceracchi correspondence in the Jefferson Papers at the Library of Congress; correspondence with Professor Ulysse Desportes of Hollins College and Miss Clara Dentler of Florence; Boyd 15:363–4; Bush, 1976, 33–36.

6. The life portrait of Jefferson painted in December of 1791 by Charles Willson Peale in Philadelphia. Independence National Historical Park.

6. THE PORTRAIT BY CHARLES WILLSON PEALE

Independence National Historical Park

MEDIUM: As is characteristic of the portraits painted for exhibition in the Peale Museum, this oil on canvas, measuring 23.4 x 19 inches, was painted for framing in an oval, with the ground extending only to the limits of the unframed area.

AUTHORSHIP: Although traditionally regarded as the life portrait, the painting that hung in Independence Hall throughout most of the latter half of the nineteenth century and the first half of the twentieth was classified by Kimball in 1944 as "an early copy, by a hand other than that" of Charles Willson Peale or his son Rembrandt, because of stylistic considerations based on an examination of both the surface and radiographs of the painting. After an identical decision on the related painting now at the Huntington Art Gallery, Kimball made it clear that he felt that the life portrait was to be regarded as lost. This decision was followed by Charles Coleman Sellers in his comprehensive study of Peale's work in 1952. That same year, however, Elizabeth Jones, then Chief Conservator of the Fogg Art Museum, removed from the canvas the repainting applied during the "restorations" of 1873–4, 1896 and 1918–19, and revealed for the first time in over half a century the original likeness. Study of this painting by Anne Clapp, who as a former Conservator of the Independence Hall Collections is thoroughly familiar with at least a hundred of Peale's Museum portraits, convinced her that the painting was indeed the work of Charles Willson Peale and one with all the earmarks of having been executed from life. Examination of X-rays of the canvas taken after the 1952 cleaning confirmed this conclusion. These considerations, added to the knowledge that this painting is now known to be that which hung originally in the Peale Museum, where its founder attempted to adhere to his "invariable rule . . . never to part with any original picture," restore this painting once again to its proper place among the life portraits of Jefferson.

CHRONOLOGY: The inscription on the earliest surviving engraving of this portrait dates the original painting to 1791. That it was painted in December of that year is established by the two letters written to arrange for Jefferson's sitting. These letters are undated but were copied into Peale's letterbooks following the last dated entry for that year—2 December 1791. It may well be that Jefferson visited the Peale household for this sitting not long before 16 December, and that it was Peale's enthusiastic proselytizing of his belief that painting should be part of the essential education of every young American that prompted Jefferson to purchase on that date a "box of paints and pencils for Maria." The task of sitting for his 50-year-old friend whose interests and objectives were so congenial to his, in the fascinating hodge-podge of science and fine art in the cluster of museum buildings at Third and Lombard Street in Philadelphia, must have been a pleasant one for the 48-year-old secretary of state.

HISTORY: Undoubtedly the painting took its place immediately after its completion among the distinguished portraits that hung in the Peale Museum. It is listed in the catalogue of 1795, just after its removal with the rest of Peale's collection, to Philosophical Hall. Late in the summer of 1800 when the Museum expanded into the upper floor of the Pennsylvania State House (Independence Hall), the painting took its place there. In 1827 the portrait was again moved, with the body of Peale's collection, to the Philadelphia Arcade. Under various proprietors the painting remained with the Museum collection until its dispersal in the sale of 1854, when the *Jefferson* was purchased for the City of Philadelphia by Mr. P. E. Erben. From 1855 until 1958 the portrait was almost continuously exhibited, along with the likenesses of other distinguished American patriots, in the room at Independence Hall in which the subjects of these paintings had passed their most momentous resolution as members of the Continental Congress. On permanent loan to the Independence National Historical Park, the portraits were removed in 1958 from Independence Hall to make possible the restoration of the building to its appearance in 1776.

CONDITION: This portrait's condition has suffered considerably during its career of public exhibition. Cleaned in 1873 or 1874 of a covering of copal varnish, the portrait seems not to have undergone major restoration until 1896 when John Wilkinson described the portrait as "nothing but a mass of flakes clinging to the canvas by an edge and a thread," and he relined and heavily repainted its surface. In 1918–19 Pasquale Farina complained of the unskillful work of his predecessors and apparently not only cleaned but also repainted the portrait himself. In 1950 Russell Quandt, Conservator at the Corcoran Gallery, was given permission to retouch some of the most badly darkened areas of repaint before the painting was exhibited in the Washington Sesquicentennial Exhibition. The painting's most important restoration, however, was carried out by Elizabeth Jones in May of 1952 when the painting was again relined and several layers of the repaint were removed. Only those areas where original paint was missing were inpainted at that time.

ICONOGRAPHIC IMPORTANCE: Not only has this portrait been exhibited publically almost continuously since its creation, but the engravings that copied it in 1795 and early in 1800 made it the first of Jefferson's likenesses to be distributed commercially through prints. Thus Charles Willson Peale's fresh and sympathetic portrayal of Jefferson has persistently shaped the public's visual conception of America's first Secretary of State.

COPIES: The painting at the Huntington Art Gallery, with a provenance that traces it to John Conduit of Newark, New Jersey, and the painting owned in 1942 by Arthur Meeker are the only known copies of the likeness executed in paint. William Birch completed an engraving of this portrait in time to enter a "proof print" of it in the 1795 exhibition of the Columbianum, but no copy of it is known to have survived. On 10 January 1800 James Akin and William Harrison, Jr., issued a stipple engraving of Peale's portrait (Stauffer 17). The portrait was issued as an etching in 1895 by E. F. Faber.

REFERENCES: Bowen, 1892, 487; Hart, 1898, 47; Kimball, 1944, 507–9; Charles

Coleman Sellers, *Charles Willson Peale*, Philadelphia, 1947, II, 41; Charles Coleman Sellers, *Portraits and Miniatures by Charles Willson Peale*, Philadelphia, 1952, 110; reports from Anne Clapp and David H. Wallace; Bush, 1976, 36–40; Cunningham, 1981, 4–7, 133.

7. THE PORTRAIT BY WILLIAM JOSEPH WILLIAMS

Unlocated

MEDIUM: The low price of this likeness and Jefferson's reference to the artist's work as a "drawing" suggest that, like Williams's surviving portrait of Washington, this was executed with pastel crayon on paper.

AUTHORSHIP: Jefferson's account book records only that he "Pd Williams for drawing [his] portrait 14D." It was Kimball who first suggested that the artist was William Joseph Williams. This attribution is almost certainly correct, since Williams was the only portraitist with this surname active in this period and since it is now known that at about the time of this portrait William Joseph Williams passed through Philadelphia en route from New York to Richmond.

CHRONOLOGY: The drawing was probably executed on 12 July 1792 in Philadelphia—the date of Jefferson's payment to Williams as recorded in the account book—unless we accept the Williams family tradition that numerous sittings were required for the completion of the pastelist's comparable portrait of Washington. It is possible that the payment dates only the last of many sittings or, since Jefferson set out from Philadelphia the following day for Monticello, that the payment, made with a number of others,

The portrait of George Washington by William Joseph Williams, artist of the undiscovered portrait of Jefferson executed in July of 1792 in Philadelphia. The Alexandria-Washington Lodge.

22

was merely among those for services rendered earlier that summer that he settled before his departure. The lost portrait, executed when Williams was 33 years of age, pictured Jefferson at 49 as secretary of state.

HISTORY: At its completion the portrait, as Jefferson's payment makes clear, went into his possession. It has never been determined whether it remained under his care in the Monticello collections or passed immediately into other hands. Nothing of its subsequent history is known.

CONDITION: The paucity of information concerning this likeness suggests its early destruction. But despite the ephemeral nature of pastel, it is possible that this portrait still reposes, unidentified, in some American collection.

ICONOGRAPHIC IMPORTANCE: Williams's candid portrayal of Washington suggests that his likeness of Jefferson was a frank and unflattering depiction that would be of interest to students of Jefferson. It seems certain, however, that its viewers were never numerous nor memorably appreciative, for the Williams pastel is among the most forgotten and uninfluential of Jefferson's portraits.

COPIES: No likeness is known that might have been derived from this portrait.

REFERENCES: Hart, 1898, 48; Kimball, 1944, 510; John Hill Morgan and Mantle Fielding, *The Life Portraits of Washington*, Philadelphia, 1931, 201; Bush, 1976, 40–41.

8. The life portrait of Jefferson drawn by James Sharples in 1797 in Philadelphia. The City Art Gallery, Bristol, England.

8. THE PORTRAIT BY JAMES SHARPLES

The City Art Gallery, Bristol, England

MEDIUM: As with most of the Sharples likenesses, the Jefferson profile was drawn with the help of the physiognotrace on a thick soft-grained wooly-textured gray paper measuring 7 x 9 inches. The subject's features were then added to this outline in pastel crayon manufactured by Sharples himself, finely powdered and applied with a brush.

AUTHORSHIP: Previous students of Jefferson's portraiture have dismissed the Sharples portrait with the comment that no documentary evidence exists to prove that the likeness was taken from life. Yet since Jefferson was in Philadelphia at a time when many of his distinguished colleagues were sitting for portraits by Sharples, since there is no extant likeness from which this pastel could have been derived, and since the physiognotrace process presupposes a life sitting, there is every reason to believe that Sharples's likeness was created in Jefferson's presence. Of the two examples of this *Jefferson* with histories tracing them to the collection in the hands of the Sharples family at the time of James Sharples's death, one in the Independence Hall collection, and one at the City Art Gallery of Bristol, England, the latter has been generally ignored in preference to the better-known example of the portrait at Independence Hall. A comparison of these two profiles, however, suggests that it is the Bristol example that most deserves our attention. It appears to be not only conceived more freely, more spontaneously and in more depth, but in specific details portrays Jefferson more accurately. In the Independence Hall profile the hair is conventionalized: vague curls suggest a wig—a characterization foreign both to Jefferson and to the Bristol portrait, which depicts Jefferson's hair as straight, falling naturally over his ear and ending in a queue, which is misunderstood in the Philadelphia pastel. In the Bristol example the eye not only seems more alert than in the Independence Hall likeness in which the eyelid is heavier, but the whole countenance is more intense and responsive than the flatter, more wooden features of the Independence Hall profile. The Bristol complexion is also convincing, not simply rouged-on as in the Philadelphia example. The costume of the Bristol portrait is suggestive and spontaneous; the profile in Philadelphia depicts the clothing in the more conventionalized and thorough detail of the copyist. In the Bristol example the jabot is only summarized and suggested, as it would have to have been at a sitting in which Sharples, as was his custom, worked with great speed. In the Independence Hall example the jabot is a conventionalization executed in the detailed manner of the copyist. The Bristol example shows a more subtle profile, while the Independence Hall example portrays the profile in what appears to be an exaggeration. Finally the provenance itself would suggest that the Bristol example is the life portrait, for it is likely that the pastels delineated from life would have remained with Sharples's widow, who carried out her husband's ambition of placing his American portraits in a permanent collection, while their competent copies would more logically be those given to her stepson Felix, who remained in America.

25

CHRONOLOGY: Jefferson and James Sharples could not have come into contact with each other until March of 1797 when Jefferson was in Philadelphia for eleven days for his inauguration as vice president. But it is likely that, instead of being executed during this brief and busy period, the pastel was drawn sometime between the vice president's return to the temporary capital on the 11th of May and his departure for Monticello on the 6th of July of the same year. By early autumn Sharples and his family had left Philadelphia for New York, where they remained at least through the greater part of 1799. After making a tour of New England and the middle states in 1800, they returned to England the following year. That the portrait dates to 1797 when both Jefferson and Sharples are known to have been in Philadelphia, rather than to any conjectural visit of the Sharpleses to the temporary capital while Jefferson was there early in 1800, is confirmed not only by the fact that the costume and the hair suggest the earlier date but also by the reasonableness of the assumption that Jefferson would have been added to the Sharples collection of distinguished Americans at the earliest opportunity. During this first journey to America, Sharples was under the responsibility of creating a reputation for himself and thus was at the height of his artistic ability. In his mid-forties at the time of this pastel, Sharples depicted Jefferson at 54.

HISTORY: After James Sharples's death during a second residence in America in 1811, his young widow, Ellen, returned with many of the portraits from his collection, including his *Jefferson,* to England. The profile remained in her care there until her death in 1849, when the collection it was a part of was bequeathed to the Royal West of England Academy in Bristol. In recent years these pastels have been on permanent loan to the City Art Gallery of Bristol.

CONDITION: Considering the fragility of portraits in pastel, this profile has survived in good condition.

ICONOGRAPHIC IMPORTANCE: Even if one accepts Hart's evaluation of the Sharples likeness as being "deficient in character and individuality," as the earliest portrait of Jefferson as vice president and as a likeness that has been publically exhibited in its many versions in both England and America almost continuously since its completion, it has had an extensive and admiring audience.

COPIES: The profile at Independence Hall, which duplicates the life portrait at Bristol, came into the Independence Hall collections in 1874 as a gift to the City of Philadelphia from F. M. Etting, who purchased it from Murray Harrison. Harrison had apparently acquired it from the Winder family, who received it with a much larger collection of Sharples portraits from James Sharples's son, Felix, as collateral on a loan. The pastel once owned by Miss Ima Hogg of Houston, Texas, is from a hand other than that which drew the profiles in Philadelphia and Bristol, but its relationship to the drawing of this likeness by Ellen Sharples, now also at Bristol, suggests that it is the

26

production of one of the younger members of the Sharples family. The outline drawing of this portrait, mentioned in Mrs. Sharples's diary, has not been found.

REFERENCES: Bowen, 1892, 487; Hart, 1898, 47; Kimball, 1944, 498; Katharine McCook Knox, *The Sharples*, New Haven, 1930; John Hill Morgan and Mantle Fielding, *The Life Portraits of Washington*, Philadelphia, 1931, 359–398; Bush, 1976, 42–45.

Thomas Jefferson
A Philosopher a Patriote and a Friend
Dessiné par son Ami Tadée Kosciuszko.
Et Gravé par M.ᵉ Sokolnicki

9. The aquatint of Jefferson printed by Michel Sokolnicki in Paris before the end of 1799 from the aquarelle (now lost) that was painted from life in Philadelphia by Tadeusz Kościuszko most probably in April of 1798. The Yale University Art Gallery.

9. THE PORTRAIT BY TADEUSZ KOŚCIUSZKO

Unlocated

MEDIUM: The lost portrait, of which we have no record other than Sokolnicki's print, most probably was executed, as is Kościuszko's comparable profile of William Bedlow, as a miniature aquarelle painted on circular paper.

AUTHORSHIP: The inscription of the aquatint makes the attribution of the original likeness to Kościuszko unequivocal. And though Kimball felt that this portrait represented Jefferson "at an age far greater than" that of his last meeting with Kościuszko and thus could "not have been from life," not only do the costume and queue suggest its placement in the context of likenesses executed during Jefferson's vice presidency, but the fact that Sokolnicki's aquatint of the portrait could only have been published in Paris between the time of Kościuszko's return there in 1798 and Sokolnicki's departure to his new command in the Second Polish Legion on the Danube at the end of 1799, make a dating of the portrait to the period of Kościuszko's Philadelphia residence not only possible, but necessary. That the portrait was taken from life is further supported by the evidence of Kościuszko's frequent opportunities to portray Jefferson during their friendship in Philadelphia and by the fact that no likeness survives that could have been the source of this profile.

CHRONOLOGY: Kościuszko had been in Philadelphia since August when Jefferson returned to that city in December of 1797 as vice president. Whether the two men then resumed an acquaintance made in Philadelphia in the beginning years of the Revolution, or, as seems more likely, met for the first time, a friendship developed between them in the early months of 1798, which led Jefferson to call the Polish patriot "the purest son of liberty of . . . all." The portrait that Kościuszko painted of Jefferson most probably dates to April of 1798 when Jefferson was so often involved in the administration of the Pole's business affairs. It is most likely that it was during these preparations for Kościuszko's return to Europe, and certainly before Jefferson's parting with him on May 4th, that the portrait, depicting Jefferson at 55—only three years older than the artist—was completed as a memento of their friendship.

HISTORY: Kościuszko must have carried the portrait directly to Paris in 1798, where it was put into the hands of Michel Sokolnicki, Kościuszko's compatriot, friend, military aid and fellow artist, who completed the surviving aquatint copy of the portrait before the end of the following year. Nothing further is known of the original portrait's history except that in 1829 it may have been in the possession of another Polish engraver—Antoine Oleszcynski—who, most probably in Paris, appears to have copied the likeness directly from the life portrait. The statement by Gardner that Kościuszko's "pastel portrait" of Jefferson is "preserved among Poland's national relics" has never been verified and is presumably based on a misidentification of one of the Sokolnicki aquatints as the original likeness.

CONDITION: The original of this likeness may still survive, unidentified, in some European collection.

ICONOGRAPHIC IMPORTANCE: Judging from the competence of extant portraits by Kościuszko, the distortions of his image of Jefferson seem more a result of exaggerations in the transcription of it into the aquatint by Sokolnicki rather than the inferiority of the original image. In July of 1816 William Thornton complained to Jefferson of the "injustice" of the portrait: ". . . nothing can be so bad," he wrote, "and when I saw it, I did not wonder that he lost Poland—not that it is necessary a Genl. should be a Painter, but he should be a man of such Sense as to discover that he is not a Painter." Oleszcynski's 1829 copy of the portrait was less a caricature and was used to represent Jefferson in biographical works published in France shortly after the completion of the new engraving. But the Kościuszko image, in Europe as well as in America, seems never to have been a popular or widely circulated one.

COPIES: Michel Sokolnicki's aquatint of 1798 or 1799 survives in rare prints. The engraving by Antoine Oleszcynski is found re-engraved by Porret in the *Galerie Napoléon* and by Clerget (Carson 1112 and 1118).

REFERENCES: Bowen, 1892, 488; Hart, 1898, 48; Kimball, 1944, 527; Helen Comstock, "Kosciuszko's Portrait of Thomas Jefferson," *The Connoisseur*, Vol. CXXXIII, No. 536 (March 1954), pp. 142–3; Correspondence with His Excellency M. Michel Sokolnicki of Ankara, Turkey; Monica M. Gardner, *Kosciuszko, A Biography*, New York, 1920, 180; Merrill D. Peterson, *The Jefferson Image in the American Mind*, New York, 1960, 508, cites "Arthur Krock's column, New York Times, 21 June 1938"; Bush, 1976, 45–48.

10. THE PORTRAIT BY ROBERT FIELD

The New-York Historical Society

MEDIUM: This unfinished portrait, painted in watercolors on cardboard, measures 9.8 x 13.8 inches.

AUTHORSHIP: The inscription on the lower edge of the face of this painting, in what has been identified as Field's hand, reads: "T. JEFFERSON. Painted by R. Field." The notes on the portrait's provenance, inscribed on the verso of the painting by a subsequent owner, also identify Field as the portrait's artist. Field's hand, in fact, is so evident in this watercolor that the closest student of this artist's work has stated that "there can be no doubt whatever that this exceedingly beautiful portrait is by Field, and an original from life." Yet previous students of Jefferson's life portraits, finding no documentary evidence that Jefferson sat to Field, have passed over this portrait in their ordering of the life likenesses. But the failure to find a likeness in an extensive study of Jefferson's portraits from which this watercolor might be derived supports what is so forcefully suggested by the immediacy and freshness of the likeness itself: that it was executed in Jefferson's presence.

CHRONOLOGY: Although the portrait was traditionally said to have been painted soon after Jefferson's inauguration as president as a study for a large portrait that was never executed, Piers accepted it as an independent work, since "it differs in no essentials from the artist's other watercolors except in being unfinished," and dated it, because of the youthfulness of the representation, "not later than 1797." That year, however, is the earliest, rather than the latest possible, date of its execution, though the youthfulness of the portrayal does suggest a date early in Jefferson's vice presidency when Field and Jefferson were in Philadelphia together for the first time. That it was painted in Philadelphia rather than in Jefferson's first years as president after Field had moved to Washington is also suggested by the descent of the painting through Charles Chauncy, a Philadelphia lawyer and one of the founders of the Pennsylvania Academy of the Fine Arts.

HISTORY: From the artist the painting went to his friend, Charles Chauncy, who left it to Thomas S. Mitchell. Mitchell presented it to Thomas J. Miles, who had it in his possession for about sixty years. He left it to his son, Colonel Thomas Carswell Miles, from whom it passed to J. Fred Pierson, who sold it to the New-York Historical Society in 1923.

CONDITION: The paper and pigment have faded considerably. The loss of color has given a startling prominence to the Chinese white on the eyes. Much of the modeling has been lost in the face as a result of prolonged exposure to light. A slight repair has been made to the left of the drapery, and the lower left corner of the painting is defaced by a clipping bearing Jefferson's franking signature and a postmark.

ICONOGRAPHIC IMPORTANCE: Never copied and seldom reproduced even in recent years, Field's portrait is the finest of the little-known portraits of Jefferson.

31

10. Robert Field's life portrait of Jefferson painted in Philadelphia about 1798. The New-York Historical Society.

COPIES: Although Field's own image of Jefferson was presumably never copied, in 1807 Field was himself to engrave, in what Piers has called his "best plate," the most handsome and important of the multitude of prints derived from Gilbert Stuart's second life portrait of Jefferson.

REFERENCES: Kimball, 1944, 498; Harry Piers, *Robert Field*, New York, 1927, 186–7, facing 190, 195; *Catalogue of American Portraits in The New-York Historical Society*, New York, 1941, 159. The statement about this portrait attributed to Jefferson on page 19 of Orland and Courtney Campbell, *The Lost Portraits of Thomas Jefferson*, Amherst College, 1959, does not appear in the original of the letter cited there; Bush, 1976, 48–50.

11. The portrait of Jefferson painted from life by Charles Peale Polk at Monticello in the first week of November 1799. Mr. Victor D. Spark, New York City.

11. THE PORTRAIT BY CHARLES PEALE POLK

Mr. Victor D. Spark, New York City

MEDIUM: The portrait is painted in oils on canvas and measures 26.8 x 28.2 inches.

AUTHORSHIP: When a version of this painting was submitted to the exhibition of historical portraiture during the Centennial Celebration of Washington's Inauguration, it was attributed to Charles Willson Peale by the exhibition's Committee on Art. Students objected to this attribution before the printing of Bowen's catalogue, and six years later Charles Henry Hart identified Charles Peale Polk as the painter of the portrait. While Polk's work has obvious similarities to that of his more competent uncle, Charles Willson Peale, in whose household he was reared after the death of his parents, the younger painter's style had matured by the time of this portrait into an expression individual enough to make the identification of his work possible on stylistic grounds. The fact that the costume and countenance portrayed in the portrait date to the time when Polk is known to have traveled to Monticello to paint Jefferson affirms not only Polk's authorship of the likeness but also its place among the life portraits.

CHRONOLOGY: Polk, who spent the winter of 1799–1800—at 32 years of age—painting portraits in Richmond, arrived at Monticello on 3 November 1799 bearing a letter from Madison introducing him as a "portrait Painter and a kinsman of Mr. Peale . . ." and stating that he was visiting "Monticello with a wish to be favored with a few hours of your sitting for his pencil." Polk's arrival is documented by Jefferson's notation in his Summary Journal of Letters of the receipt of this letter "by Mr. Polk" and by Jefferson's reference to the painter in his reply to Madison of 22 November. The portrait most probably was begun on the day of Polk's arrival—3 November 1799—and was completed on November 5th, according to the painter's own notice published in *The Virginia Gazette and General Advertiser* on November 18th. The painting depicts Jefferson at 56 in one of his cherished Monticello interludes from his public responsibilities as vice president.

HISTORY: Hart recorded the tradition that the painting was painted under the commission of Major Issac Hite of the Shenandoah Valley, Virginia, and that it descended to his grandson, Madison Hite, Jr., who, during the Civil War, deposited it in Baltimore with a number of other paintings for safekeeping, though he never recovered it. Linda Crocker Simmons convincingly argues in her work on Charles Peale Polk that this painting is the one purchased before 1962 by Victor Spark, an art dealer in New York City, from a man who claimed it came from a family in Washington, D.C. It was in Mr. Spark's care when Miss Simmons's research elevated it to the position of life portrait in the catalogue produced to accompany the traveling exhibition of the work of Polk that opened in 1981 in the Corcoran Gallery of Art. From the Corcoran this exhibition traveled to the Abbey Aldrich Rockefeller Folk Art Center, Williamsburg, Virginia (1981), the Dayton Art Institute, Dayton, Ohio (1982), the Hunter Museum of Art,

Chattanooga, Tennessee (1982), and the Heritage Plantation of Sandwich, Massachusetts (1982). It was later shown at the Virginia Museum of Fine Arts, Richmond, in an exhibition titled "Painting in the South, 1564–1980" (1983–84), and in 1984 in both the Birmingham Museum of Art, Birmingham, Alabama, and the National Academy of Design, New York City.

CONDITION: A photograph of the painting before cleaning and relining while in Mr. Spark's care shows damage to the painting in the left background and a tear to the left of Jefferson's head. In both instances these show only minor loss of paint.

ICONOGRAPHIC IMPORTANCE: Polk's inability "to Obtain business in the line of [his] Profession," the "*extreme distress*" of his family, and his appeals to Jefferson in the early years of his presidency for "some Subordinate appointment," all suggest that Polk's portraits were regarded by his contemporaries as inferior works. His depiction of Jefferson was never widely known until the 1981 Corcoran exhibition and the many exhibitions that followed.

COPIES: *The Virginia Gazette and General Advertiser* for 18 November 1799 carried Charles Peale Polk's notice that ". . . he has for sale, A few copies of General Washington, and Thomas Jefferson, Esq. from an original Portrait by myself, finished at Monticello on the 5th instant. . . ." At least three paintings duplicating this portrait, all of them probably replicas, survive. The portrait previously thought to be that from life, now owned by the American Scenic and Historic Preservation Society, Yonkers, New York, as the bequest of Alexander Smith Cochran, was once owned by Robert O. Grayson. The portrait given to the University of Virginia by J. William Middendorf II was once owned by John Kenneth Byard of New York City. A third replica, descending in the family of Amelia Field Clay, survives in a private collection.

REFERENCES: Bowen, 1892, 487; Hart, 1898, 48; Kimball, 1944, 498; American Scenic and Historic Preservation Society *Bulletin,* Vol. 1, No. 3 (Sept. 1929), 5, 11; *Antiques,* Vol. LXII, No. 6 (Dec. 1952), 433; Charles Peale Polk to Thomas Jefferson, 28 February 1802 and James Madison to Thomas Jefferson, 2 November 1799, respectively in the Jefferson Papers at the Library of Congress and the Library of Knox College; correspondence of Jacquelin Davison and S. C. March and Charles Henry Hart in the Frick Art Reference Library; correspondence of Mrs. Imogen C. Riely; 1968 correspondence of Braxton Davenport and John Cook Wyllie in the University of Virginia Library; Bush, 1976, 50–53; Linda Crocker Simmons, *Charles Peale Polk, 1776–1822, A Limner and His Likenesses,* Washington, D.C., 1981, frontispiece, 10, 66–67.

12. THE FIRST LIFE PORTRAIT BY REMBRANDT PEALE

The White House

MEDIUM: In this oil on diagonal twill canvas, the lean use of paint more typical of Rembrandt Peale has given way, partly because of the roughness of the canvas, to a richer impaste. The paint was applied with the directness, spontaneity and boldness that characterize the best expositions of his early style. The placement of the figure on the canvas, the simple background and the obvious shading are all derived directly from his father's style, in which the younger Peale worked with facility and confidence until his contact with Europe.

AUTHORSHIP: Although a knowledge of this portrait until recently was restricted to those persons in direct contact with it, they seem never to have lost sight of the fact that it was painted by Rembrandt Peale. When it was purchased in the mid-nineteenth century by Charles Eaton, it was surely with the knowledge that it was a surviving part of the dispersed collections of Peale's Baltimore museum; and although the portrait bore no inscription and, apparently, no labels to indicate its author, the cataloguer of the collections of the Peabody Institute in 1900 attributed the painting to Rembrandt Peale. This attribution was unquestioned by Anna Wells Rutledge when she compiled her hand list of the Institute's collection in 1946. The evidence of style, a provenance that traces the painting to the original collections in Peale's Baltimore museum, and, most especially, the identification of the original likeness's author on its earliest engravings confirm that Rembrandt Peale was its creator. That it was painted from life is established by the fact that it is the ultimate source of the numerous prints that made this the most extensively distributed image of Jefferson during his presidency, and also by Jefferson's request of 21 March 1801 that Rembrandt "make a copy of the portrait he took of [him]. . . ."

CHRONOLOGY: Painted sometime after Jefferson's arrival in Philadelphia in late December of 1799 and his departure for Monticello in the middle of May 1800, the portrait depicts the 57-year-old vice president on the threshold of the presidency of the United States. Though Rembrandt Peale himself had just turned 22, he was a veteran portraitist, having painted Washington successfully five years earlier. The young painter was at the zenith of his native style, a style that was to undergo what was not a thoroughly happy sophistication during his study in Europe two years later. Rembrandt Peale had just returned to Philadelphia after an abortive attempt to establish an art museum in Baltimore, and since it was September before a card appeared in the newspapers informing Philadelphians of the removal of Rembrandt's studio to Mulberry Court, it may well have been at his temporary painting rooms at 110 Walnut Street that Jefferson sat for him. The portrait was most probably completed in a single sitting; two were required at most.

HISTORY: As part of Peale's original gallery of paintings at his Baltimore museum,

12. The life portrait of Jefferson painted in Philadelphia early in 1800 by Rembrandt Peale. The White House.

the painting stayed there with the collection under the custodianship of the painter's brother Rubens, to whom the building and its contents were sold in 1822. When Rubens severed his ties to the collection, over ten years later, the painting was part of the effects of Rembrandt's original museum, which survived many moves, at least two fires and a number of uninterested proprietors. The last of these was Charles Getz, who in 1854 was privately selling the remnants of the painting collection that had originally hung in Peale's Baltimore Museum. At the time, Charles J. M. Eaton, 47 years old, affluent and infected with the collecting spirit, purchased the *Jefferson* and at least one other of the Peale paintings for his growing collection. The painting remained part of Eaton's vast and uncatalogued private collection until his death in 1893, when it was presented by Eaton's daughters to the Peabody Institute, over which their father had presided as president. After scholarly attention was turned to Jefferson's portraits late in the nineteenth century, it was probably Charles Henry Hart who first recognized that the 1800 life portrait of Jefferson by Peale was unlocated, for he circulated photographs of engravings of it in an unsuccessful attempt to find the original. William J. Campbell admitted in the catalogue of portraits brought together for the centennial of Washington's inauguration that although this painting was among the most important of Jefferson's portraits, he had been unable to trace the original. Eleven years later Hart was forced to state that the original portrait was "known at the present day only through contemporary engravings. . . . ," Lipscomb and Bergh failed to find it in their search for Jefferson portraits in 1903. John Hill Morgan concluded in 1930 that Peale's earliest life portrait of Jefferson was "known only by engravings . . . ," and in 1937 H. E. Dickson's study of engravings derived from the life portrait concluded that the "portrait seems to have disappeared." The painting remained unknown to the committee that assembled the exhibition of portraits for Jefferson's bicentennial in 1943 in the National Gallery, and in the comprehensive study of Jefferson's portraits that resulted from this exhibition, Fiske Kimball searched without success for Peale's earliest portrait of Jefferson and finally had to pass over it as one of "the paintings reputed to stand back of various engravings of which we know nothing further." In 1953 when Rosenberger reproduced the life portraits in his *Jefferson Reader*, the 1800 Peale portrait was still missing. It was not until 1959 that the Peabody portrait was identified as the long sought after life portrait of 1800. It was then purchased from the Peabody Institute by Paul Mellon and presented to the White House.

CONDITION: The portrait has survived in extraordinarily good condition. The creases caused by the unbeveled edge of the stretcher and a small three-corner tear in the area of Jefferson's left cheek are the only notable damage. When the patch that had been used to repair the tear was cleared away, Elizabeth Packard of the Walter's Art Gallery, who directed the cleaning and relining of the painting in 1960, discovered almost all of the original surface intact so that the restoration demanded virtually no new paint.

ICONOGRAPHIC IMPORTANCE: Among the earliest and most penetrating likenesses of

Jefferson, this portrait is unrivalled in having played a more significant iconographic role during Jefferson's lifetime than any other portrait. Shortly after its completion it became the prototype of a widely distributed series of American and European engravings. The American public received through these engravings their first visual image of the man they were twice to choose as President. Peale's arresting portrait thus served as an important and convincing item of political propaganda. No portrait of Jefferson, with the exception of the one painted in 1805 by Gilbert Stuart, which later eclipsed that of Peale in the public mind, seems to have been so frequently copied. This was, in fact, so thoroughly the image of Jefferson impressed upon the senses of the American people that political cartoonists copied its lineaments in order to make the Jefferson of their satires immediately recognizable. It was the ultimate source of the French and English image of the man who, next to Franklin, most nearly symbolized the New World in the eyes of the Old.

COPIES: Although Jefferson ordered a replica of this portrait from the painter, it was evidently never executed. The painting was first reproduced by David Edwin in a stipple engraving dated 1800 and in the following year in the same medium by Cornelius Tiebout. These two engravings, the only likenesses taken directly from the life portrait, became the sources for at least fifty further versions of this portrait that were painted, engraved and lithographed in the nineteenth century. Among the notable likenesses derived from this life portrait through these two prints is the handsome crayon drawing by Bouch dated 1801 and drawn from Tiebout's 1801 engraving. This crayon, now owned by Abbot Low Moffat of Princeton, New Jersey, was itself copied in the engraving by August Gaspard Louis Boucher, later the Baron Desnoyers, who created the image of Jefferson which "is the type followed in France even to-day." This French engraving in turn served as the immediate source for the oil portrait by an anonymous copyist that is now owned by Francis L. Barton. The Desnoyers engraving also was copied in a line engraving by William Holl the younger in England and, with further derivatives there, became perhaps the most important of the British images of Jefferson. One of these appears on a portrait plaque of Liverpool creamware. The head in the full-length painting of Jefferson by Caleb Boyle, now at Lafayette College, is also ultimately derived from Peale's life portrait of 1800 through the David Edwin engraving.

REFERENCES: The painting itself is most faithfully reproduced in the full color print published by the Princeton University Press in 1960; Bowen, 1892, 478–489; Hart, 1898, 51; Kimball, 1944, 498; Peabody Institute Gallery of Art, *List of Works of Art on Exhibition Including the Collections of John W. McCoy and Charles J. M. Eaton*, Baltimore, 1900, 27; Anna Wells Rutledge, *List of Works of Art in the Collection of The Peabody Institute*, Baltimore, 1949, 17; Wilbur H. Hunter, Jr., *Rendezvous for Taste, Peale's Baltimore Museum*, Baltimore, 1956, 6; Alfred L. Bush, "Rembrandt Peale's Earliest Life Portrait of Thomas Jefferson," unpublished typescript; Maxine Cheshire, "Portrait Used by Jefferson in Campaign Is Acquired," *The Washington Post*, Dec. 9, 1962; Julian P. Boyd,

"Jefferson's Portrait" in "Letters to the Editor," *The Washington Post,* Dec. 17, 1962, Al8; *Joséphine Parures, Décors et Jardins, Rueil-Malmaison,* 1969, 10; Robert Macauley, *Transfer Designs on Anglo American Pottery,* No. 228; *The White House, An Historic Guide,* Washington, D.C., 1963, 54; Adams, 1976, 194–195; Bush, 1976, 53–58; Cunningham, 1981, 11–12, 14, 22–53, 67, 87, 109, 119, 139.

13. The mezzotint engraved, most probably by David Edwin, from the portrait of Jefferson that Edward Savage painted from life in Philadelphia early in 1800. The Historical Society of Pennsylvania.

13. THE PORTRAIT BY EDWARD SAVAGE

Unlocated

MEDIUM: The inscription on the surviving mezzotint copy of the lost original of this likeness, which refers to Savage as the painter of the portrait, and the fact that Savage's portraits were typically executed in oils on canvas indicate that the original of this likeness was also in this medium and may have measured, as do comparable portraits by Savage, about 30 x 25 inches.

AUTHORSHIP: The inscription on the mezzotint engraving of this portrait ascribes the original painting to Edward Savage. But without documentary evidence that Jefferson sat for Savage, previous students of Jefferson's life portraits have ignored this likeness. Yet since Savage and Jefferson were residents of Philadelphia together, were acquainted with each other, and since Savage was at the time painting portraits for his gallery of distinguished Americans, it is reasonable to believe that during the same year that Jefferson granted sittings to Polk, Rembrandt Peale and Stuart, he would also have been willing to sit to a painter ranked by his contemporaries with Copley, West and Trumbull as among the "American geniuses of the present time." That no portrait has been found that could have been used as the source for this likeness further supports its position among the life portraits.

CHRONOLOGY: The date of Savage's first acquaintance with Jefferson is unrecorded, but since the painter did not settle in Philadelphia until 1795, they presumably could not have met until Jefferson's return to the temporary capital in 1797 as vice president. And since it was not until the winter of 1799–1800 that Philadelphia's portraitists, spurred by Jefferson's candidacy for the presidency, began requesting sittings, it is most probable that Savage's life portrait was painted not long before work on the mezzotint print of it, issued on the first of June 1800, was begun. Certainly in costume and countenance this *Jefferson* is similar to the other portraits dated to that year. It was about this time that Philadelphians were invited to Savage's "New Exhibition Gallery of Paintings" at No. 70 South Fourth Street for an exhibition of "original American Historical Paintings taken from the most interesting subjects. . . ." Thus it may have been in Savage's painting rooms at this address that Jefferson posed for the portrait that could have been part of this April exhibition. Jefferson, in fact, may well have given Savage his first commission to frame prints for the Monticello collections at the time of the sitting, since on the 12th of May 1800 he paid Savage for such a service at a time when the mezzotint was close to completion.

HISTORY: As part of Savage's gallery, the painting most probably accompanied the artist in his move from Philadelphia to New York in 1801 to become part of the collection of the New-York Museum, which Savage and a partner inaugurated there. These collections were later reassembled as the Columbian Museum in Boston, where it seems most likely that the *Jefferson* was destroyed when the museum and the greater part of its contents burned in 1803.

43

CONDITION: The original painting is thought to have been burned in the 1803 fire in Boston's Columbian Museum. The exceedingly rare mezzotint of it that survives at the Historical Society of Pennsylvania is neither an early printing of the engraving nor a well-preserved copy: the surface is generally rubbed and bears a flaw at the inner edge of Jefferson's left eye.

ICONOGRAPHIC IMPORTANCE: The Savage likeness enjoyed a very brief reign. Its availability in the mezzotint version as a recent portrait of the newly elected President made its piracy by other engravers inevitable. Before the end of 1801 unauthorized versions of it appeared as frontispieces to the Newark and Boston editions of Jefferson's *Notes on the State of Virginia* and one of the volumes of James Hardie's biographical dictionary. But almost immediately the image was eclipsed by the superiority of Rembrandt Peale's 1800 likeness and the popularity of the numerous prints derived from the latter through Tiebout's engraving of February 1801. The rarity of the mezzotint is itself testimony to how rapidly and thoroughly the image fell out of favor.

COPIES: Despite the inscription on the 1800 mezzotint, which asserts that both the painting and the engraving are the work of Savage himself, Dickson's argument against Savage's competence as an engraver and his identification of David Edwin as the ghost engraver of the more important of Savage's American prints suggest that the latter is more probably the engraver of this mezzotint, which seems to be the only copy taken directly from Savage's life portrait. Only one of the 1801 piracies of the mezzotint is signed—that used as the frontispiece of the Newark edition of Jefferson's *Notes on the State of Virginia,* which bears the signature of John Scoles. Neither the engraving in the Boston edition of the *Notes* nor that in James Hardie's *The New Universal Biographical Dictionary and American Remembrancer of Departed Merit . . .* (New York, 1801; nor subsequent editions) bears indication of the identity of the engraver.

REFERENCES: Bowen, 1892, 489; Hart, 1898, 48; Kimball, 1944, 498; Louisa Dresser, "Edward Savage," *Art in America,* Vol. 40, No. 4 (Autumn 1952); Harold E. Dickson, "The Case Against Savage," *American Collector,* XIV (Jan. 1946), 6–7, 17; DAB; Jefferson to Edward Savage, 10 January 1802 in the Jefferson Papers at the Library of Congress; Bush, 1976, 58–61; Cunningham, 1981, 11–17, 20–21, 139–140, 146.

14. THE FIRST LIFE PORTRAIT BY GILBERT STUART

Unlocated

MEDIUM: Jefferson's reference to this painting as Stuart's "1st canvas portrait" of him and one "of the common size" suggests that the portrait was painted in oil on canvas and measured, as do comparable portraits by Stuart dating to this period, about 28 x 24 inches.

AUTHORSHIP: Jefferson's negotiations with Henry Dearborn for the acquisition of this portrait, the entry in Jefferson's accounts for the payment to Stuart for this 1800 likeness, and the inscriptions on the Orme and Vernor-Hood engravings of the portrait published in England in 1801, all establish Stuart's authorship of a portrait of Jefferson painted from life in 1800. Fiske Kimball's authoritative ordering, in 1944, of Stuart's portraits of Jefferson dispelled the confusion of misidentification and misdating surrounding this, the earliest of Stuart's life portraits of Jefferson, and established for the first time that the likeness is presumably preserved only in contemporary engravings.

CHRONOLOGY: Almost twenty years after the execution of this likeness, Jefferson remembered that "it was in May, 1800" that Stuart painted his first life portrait of him. Since his payment is dated 12 May 1800, it was in the early weeks of that month, most probably in Stuart's Germantown studio, just outside Philadelphia, that the sitting took place. Jefferson, at 57, was portrayed on the threshold of the presidency. Stuart, recognized even then as the greatest of America's portraitists, was 44. Although the sittings were completed at the time of the payment, the artist had not as yet "put the last hand on it, so it was left with him."

HISTORY: Since the two prints that were engraved directly from the canvas were both engraved in England, it is possible that Stuart, without Jefferson's permission, shipped the painting to London for engraving. Though Jefferson's later negotiations concerning Stuart's portraits show that he still believed the 1800 canvas to be in Stuart's possession, Stuart's reference in 1820 to "the one" *Jefferson* then in his studio—the 1805 Edgehill likeness—indicates that by then the 1800 portrait was no longer in the painter's hands. Nothing has been found to document its subsequent history.

CONDITION: Kimball suggested, since the inferiority of the likeness as reproduced in the British engravings of it supports Stuart's claim of being dissatisfied with the likeness, "that Stuart 'rubbed it out,' as he said he did one of his life portraits of Washington." It is also possible, however, that the canvas was never returned from its suppositional journey to England for engraving.

ICONOGRAPHIC IMPORTANCE: Jefferson's comment that he thought Stuart's "1st canvas portrait . . . a good one" was probably elicited by his willingness to accept, after twenty years of negotiation, any of the portraits that Stuart had painted and sold to him,

THOMAS JEFFERSON ESQ.ᴿ

14. The engraving issued by Vernor and
Hood in London on 1 October 1801, which is
most probably the most faithful surviving
representation of the lost portrait of Jefferson
painted in May of 1800 in Philadelphia by
Gilbert Stuart. The Alderman Library, The
University of Virginia.

rather than a considered evaluation of the merits of the painter's earliest likeness. The surviving engravings preserve a representation that gives ample ground to Stuart's statement of dissatisfaction with the portrait. But in its engraved form the image had a far-reaching, if brief, currency. In England, in Germany, and in America (as frontispieces to two editions of Jefferson's *Notes on the State of Virginia*) the distortions of Stuart's 1800 portrait were perpetuated for a short while before being discarded in favor of Rembrandt Peale's portrait.

COPIES: This portrait was first reproduced in a print by Edward Orme published on August 1, 1801, in London. As Courtney and Orland Campbell have correctly pointed out, the hasty and inaccurate duplication of the original canvas in this print resulted from the shortcut that Orme resorted to in producing it. Instead of delineating Stuart's *Jefferson* faithfully as a wholly new engraved portrait, Orme merely adapted a copperplate of an earlier engraving of his of Muzzio Clementi into this *Jefferson*. Engraving Jefferson's head over Clementi's, modifying the costume of the earlier portrait as little as necessary, Orme concocted a formidable pastiche of Stuart's head of Jefferson superimposed upon the slightly extended shoulders of Muzzio Clementi. On October 1st of the same year, Vernor and Hood issued their engraved version of the likeness—the only other taken directly from the life portrait and its most faithful representation. That this print was in America early in 1802 is established by the fact that it was copied as the frontispiece to the 1802 Boston edition of Jefferson's *Notes on the State of Virginia*, which in turn was copied the following year for the frontispiece to the Trenton edition of the same work. German versions of this likeness, by Mayer, Topham and Netting, are based on the Orme engraving, while subsequent British versions are derived from the Vernor-Hood print.

REFERENCES: Bowen, 1892, 483–485; Hart, 1898, 54; Kimball, 1944, 512–523; Fiske Kimball, "Gilbert Stuart's Portraits of Jefferson," *Gazette des Beaux-Arts*, 6th series, Vol. 26, 95–112 (1944); Orland and Courtney Campbell, *The Lost Portraits of Thomas Jefferson*, Amherst College, 1959, 12 (on the claim advanced by the Campbell brothers, see the related discussion and references in this catalogue under Stuart's Edgehill portrait of Jefferson); Bush, 1976, 61–64.

15. The verre églomisé portrait of Jefferson engraved from life at Monticello by A. B. Doolittle in December of 1803. The Thomas Jefferson Memorial Foundation.

15. THE PORTRAIT BY A. B. DOOLITTLE

The Thomas Jefferson Memorial Foundation

MEDIUM: Measuring 3 x 3.8 inches, this is one of the few surviving American portraits in verre églomisé. In these "profiles on gold leaf shadowed a little by hatching," as Dunlap describes them, the likeness was engraved through a ground of gold applied to a transparent glass surface. After the image was engraved and the gold outside the area of the profile cut away, the surface of the glass was covered with a black paint. Viewed through the glass, the gold profile is contrasted sharply against this black ground.

AUTHORSHIP: The portrait bears no inscription, but is stylistically identical to the verre églomisé portrait of John Adams at the American Antiquarian Society, which is inscribed: "AB Doolittle Fecit." The rarity of the use of this medium for portraits in America, the stylistic coincidence of the *Jefferson* with the Doolittle *Adams* at Worcester, and the record of Doolittle's completion of profiles of Jefferson at Monticello confirm both Doolittle's authorship of this likeness and its place among those executed from life.

CHRONOLOGY: On December 23, 1803, Jefferson recorded a payment of 15 dollars to Doolittle for three profiles. On January 7, 1804, Jefferson "gave Mr. Doolittle ord. on J. Barnes for 10. D. for profiles," and on February 10th he "gave Doolittle ord. on J. Barnes for 10. D. for profiles." The subjects of these seven profiles purchased from Doolittle by Jefferson are not recorded, but recognizing the commercial value of the President's portrait, it is most likely that the earliest sitting at Monticello for Doolittle —late in December of 1803—was for the gold profile depicting Jefferson at 60 years of age.

HISTORY: This portrait hung in the Tea Room at Monticello in Jefferson's time and must have passed to Septimia Randolph Meikleham as part of her inheritance from Jefferson, her grandfather, since "an old portrait of Jefferson on glass" is reported as being in her possession in 1883. It was part of the estate inherited by Dr. Robert Graves and his sister, Mrs. Cantrell, children of Mrs. H. P. Meikleham by a former marriage, and seems never to have left the Meikleham family until shortly before its acquisition by the Thomas Jefferson Memorial Foundation as the gift of James A. Bear, Jr.

CONDITION: Despite the fragile nature of portraits in verre églomisé, the profile is remarkably preserved with only minor portions of the black ground detached from the glass.

ICONOGRAPHIC IMPORTANCE: Jefferson's accounts, Bentley's diary and a letter of thanks from Elizabeth Trist suggest that this likeness was duplicated a number of times in the original medium, was distributed commercially by Doolittle, and was part of collections in cities as widely separated as Salem and New Orleans. And though Elizabeth Trist's insistence that her replica of the profile bore a "perfect . . . resemblance" seems more an effusive expression of gratitude to Jefferson for the gift than a candid appraisal of the accuracy of the portrait, the profile itself may have suggested something

49

characteristic enough to elicit such a response. The likeness, presumably the first from life of Jefferson as President, was apparently known only in its original medium, and, excepting such unusual occasions as the celebration of the 4th of July of 1804 when it was publicly exhibited in Salem, it was seldom viewed and remained known to a very small circle of people.

COPIES: Replicas of this verre églomisé *Jefferson* may have been carried north in the spring of 1804 by Doolittle himself. At least William Bentley, whose collection included the Doolittle verre églomisé profile of Adams, describes the decorations of the Salem Meeting House for the 4th of July of 1804 as including a portrait of Jefferson "on glass in gold." It is also almost certain that the likeness that Jefferson sent as a gift to Elizabeth Trist that same year was a further example of this portrait. Receiving the glass profile from Issac Briggs, who could transport it carefully from Washington with the fragile instruments he was carrying for the exploration of the Mississippi Territory, Elizabeth Trist responded to Jefferson's kindness extravagantly, calling the likeness "exactly yourself in short it elated the Spirits of us all to behold so perfect a resemblance of such a valued and dear friend, to me it is an inestimable treasure. . . ."

REFERENCES: Hart, 1898, 48; Kimball, 1944, 497–8; Alice Van Leer Carrick, *Shades of Our Ancestors*, Boston, 1928, 72–77; Elizabeth Trist to Jefferson, 26 November 1804 in the Alderman Library, University of Virginia; *The Diary of William Bentley*, Salem, 1911, III, 96; Colin Eisler, "Verre Églomisé and Paolo di Giovanni Fei," *Journal of Glass Studies*, Vol. III (1961), 30–37; clipping, from an unidentified newspaper of ca. 1883, titled "MRS. SEPTIMIA R. MEIKLEHAM, JEFFERSON'S GRANDDAUGHTER" in the files of The Thomas Jefferson Memorial Foundation, Inc.; Bush, 1976, 64–67; Cunningham, 1981, 135–137, 158.

16. THE PORTRAIT BY CHARLES-BALTHAZAR-JULIEN FEVRET DE SAINT-MÉMIN

The Worcester Art Museum

MEDIUM: On coarse textured paper measuring 23.13 x 17 inches covered with a pink watercolor wash, Saint-Mémin first traced Jefferson's profile with the help of the physiognotrace. The details of the subject's features were then delineated in this outline with a grey wash and black and white chalk.

AUTHORSHIP: The only inscription on the drawing as it survives is not contemporary with its execution. Not only is the likeness unmistakably the work of Saint-Mémin, however, but the prints engraved from it and purchased by Jefferson with the original drawing bear the artist's abbreviated signature. The very nature of the physiognotrace process requires that profiles drawn with this device be taken from life.

CHRONOLOGY: Jefferson's payment on 27 November 1804 for the original crayon, the copperplate engraved from this drawing, and forty-eight small engravings struck from it was most probably made, as was customary, on the day of the sitting. Jefferson, portrayed at 61, approaching the end of his first term as president and already elected for a second term, most probably sat to the 34-year-old Saint Mémin at the artist's rooms in David Shoemaker's house on F Street in Washington where the profilist's cumbersome physiognotrace device was housed.

HISTORY: Though Jefferson's daughter Maria reminded the president in February of 1804 that he had "promised us your picture if ever St. Mimin went to Washington" and noted that the artist was to be there in the "middle of this month," it was not until late in the year that St. Mémin and Jefferson were able to collaborate. While Jefferson's purchase indicates that the drawing went directly into his hands, nothing is known of its subsequent possession by him or his family. After its initial acquisition the ownership of the crayon is not recorded again until its possession, with other "important and authentic Jefferson relics," by the historian George Bancroft. The profile passed, in the nineteenth century, to the historian's son, John Chandler Bancroft, and was on loan at the Worcester Art Museum from 1901 until its purchase by that institution in 1954 from the estate of Wilder D. Bancroft.

CONDITION: Before 1901, when it came to Worcester, the right edge of the portrait had been repaired with the insertion of a rectangular patch, about 3.5 x 1.3 inches, taken from the upper right margin of the sheet. Within this patch the extreme portions of the bow in Jefferson's hair have been redrawn by a restorer. At the lower edge of the portrait, written in graphite over old blemishes—and thus long after the execution of the profile—is "Tho. Jefferson."

ICONOGRAPHIC IMPORTANCE: Saint-Mémin engraved a second copper plate of his *Jefferson* and was striking prints from it for commercial sale at the time of Jefferson's second inauguration. That Jefferson's contemporaries found these prints attractive is

51

16. The life portrait of Jefferson by Charles-Balthazar-Julien Fevret de Saint-Mémin, drawn with the help of the physiognotrace on 27 November 1804 in Washington. The Worcester Art Museum.

indicated by the many examples of them that have survived. It was this print, in fact, that Thomas Gimbrede used as the basis for his likeness of Jefferson in the apotheosis titled *Jefferson the Pride of America*, which he engraved just after Jefferson's retirement from the presidency and which Septimia R. Meikleham believed to be "a testimonial circulated by the friends of her grandfather to show their appreciation of his worth and his services to his country." Later the likeness was copied in Paris in a lithograph by Langlumé dedicated to Jefferson's friend David Warden, "ancien Consul des états Unis à Paris." Through further copies the Saint-Mémin *Jefferson* became a widely circulated and familiar image of Jefferson in France. Cherished by some of Jefferson's descendants as an especially characteristic likeness, the Saint-Mémin image was extensively distributed, in both America and France, and persistently admired.

COPIES: The original copperplate purchased by Jefferson showing the likeness circumscribed in a circle is now in the Princeton University Library, as is an example of the engravings pulled from it. The later copperplate, bearing the likeness within an oval, is owned by the Alderman Library, University of Virginia. Besides the original prints taken from the oval plate early in the nineteenth century, a thousand copies of the print were restruck from it in 1956 by the University of Virginia. The Langlumé lithograph and its various derivatives survive in the Bibliothèque Nationale. Thomas Gimbrede's apotheosis (Stauffer 1058) and the bas-relief by George Miller (in the plaster at the American Philosophical Society, which was erroneously identified by Hart as a life portrait; in a plaster owned by Mrs. J. P. Chalfant of Wilmington, Delaware; and in bronze at Monticello and the Henry Francis DuPont Winterthur Museum) are only the most notable of the many likenesses copied from the image engraved from the oval copperplate. Albert Rosenthal copied not only the original drawing in crayon in 1905 but also produced an engraved version the same year.

REFERENCES: Bowen, 1892, 486–7; Hart, 1898, 52–3; Kimball, 1944, 523–4; Howard C. Rice, Jr., "Saint-Mémin's Portrait of Jefferson," *The Princeton University Library Chronicle*, Vol. XX, No. 4 (Summer 1959), 182–192; L[ouisa] D[resser], "A Life Portrait of Thomas Jefferson," *Worcester Art Museum News Bulletin and Calendar*, Vol. XVII, No. 3 (Dec. 1951), 9–10; *A Catalogue of Portraits and Other Works of Art in the Possession of the American Philosophical Society*, Philadelphia, 1961, 53–4; correspondence with Miss Louisa Dresser; a clipping, from an unidentified newspaper of ca. 1883, titled "MRS. SEPTIMIA R. MEIKLEHAM, JEFFERSON'S GRANDDAUGHTER" in the files of The Thomas Jefferson Memorial Foundation; Edwin M. Betts and James A. Bear, Jr., editors, *The Family Letters of Thomas Jefferson*, Columbia, 1966, 256; Fawn M. Brodie, *Thomas Jefferson, An Intimate History*, New York, 1974, 378; Adams, 1976, 75, 399; Bush, 1976, 67–70; Cunningham, 1981, 81–83.

17. The portrait of Jefferson painted from life in Washington by Rembrandt Peale on the 23rd, 24th and 31st of January 1805. The New-York Historical Society.

17. THE SECOND LIFE PORTRAIT BY REMBRANDT PEALE

The New-York Historical Society

MEDIUM: Painted in oils on canvas, the portrait measures 28 x 23.8 inches.

AUTHORSHIP: Though the painting bears no inscription, Rembrandt Peale's authorship of the portrait has always been acknowledged, and the painter's father's contemporary statement that "Jefferson sat" to Rembrandt Peale for this portrait establishes its place among the life likenesses. The canvas now at the New-York Historical Society, though unquestionably from Rembrandt's hand, has at times been overlooked as portraits derived from it have been presented as the original likeness. But Kimball's confirmation of the position of this painting as the life portrait is supported not only by decisive visual considerations but also by its provenance.

CHRONOLOGY: Contemporary letters of Charles Willson Peale date with exactness the three sittings required by his son for this portrait. Jefferson sat for Rembrandt Peale in the president's residence on the 23rd, 24th and 31st of January 1805. The portrait was virtually completed in the first two sittings, the last sitting being used only to "retouch" the painting. Though Rembrandt was only 25 years of age, the portraits he had painted during the previous decade, including his first life portrait of Jefferson five years earlier, had earned him an acknowledged place among the best of America's portraitists. In the years between his first portrait of Jefferson and this likeness, Rembrandt had studied briefly at the Royal Academy in London, infusing the forthrightness of his native portrait manner with the sophistications of his European counterparts. Jefferson, at 61 years of age, is depicted in this painting shortly after his re-election to a second term as president.

HISTORY: On March 3, 1805, the eve of Jefferson's second inauguration, this portrait was displayed at a special illumination of the Peale Museum in Philadelphia. The portrait remained with the collections of the Peale Museum, in fact, until their dispersal in the 1854 sale, when it was purchased by Thomas J. Bryan. Twelve years later Mr. Bryan presented it to the New-York Historical Society.

CONDITION: In the curatorial care of The New-York Historical Society for almost a century, the portrait survives in excellent condition. The canvas was cleaned in 1938 and was relined for the first time in 1962.

ICONOGRAPHIC IMPORTANCE: Charles Willson Peale expressed both his and Rembrandt's satisfaction with the portrait, and students of Rembrandt's work have often called it his finest production. Though never engraved in the 19th century, this superb painting—almost continuously on public exhibition since its creation—has become widely admired as one of the most penetrating and memorable of Jefferson's likenesses. It is especially instructive to compare this likeness with that by the same artist five years earlier.

COPIES: Although Rembrandt advertised, on the very day it was finished, his willingness to paint replicas of this portrait, only one is known to survive: that owned by the widow of Lawrence Coolidge (to whom it had descended through Harold Jefferson Coolidge), who subsequently became Mrs. Gilbert L. Steward. About 1858 James L. Dick painted the copy that now hangs at Monticello, and Caroline Ormes Ransom executed the copy now owned by the United States Department of State sometime before July of 1881. A copy by an unidentified painter was discovered in 1927 in a Fourth Avenue bookshop in New York City and is now owned by Mr. William Marcus Greve. The copy owned by the Manufacturers Trust Company is also by an unidentified copyist.

REFERENCES: Bowen, 1892, 487; Hart, 1898, 51; Kimball, 1944, 523–525; *Catalogue of American Portraits in The New-York Historical Society,* New York, 1941, 160–1; Bush, 1976, 70–73; Cunningham, 1981; 133–134.

18. THE EDGEHILL PORTRAIT BY GILBERT STUART

The Thomas Jefferson Memorial Foundation and the National Portrait Gallery

MEDIUM: Painted in oils on a mahogany or walnut panel, the portrait measures 26.4 x 21.12 inches.

AUTHORSHIP: That the Edgehill panel is the original of Stuart's 1805 bust-size image of Jefferson is assured by the painter's statement to Martha Jefferson Randolph that he had "sent the original" to Monticello, by Jefferson's explicit instructions to Stuart that he should receive the life portrait, by the fact that it was the Edgehill panel that remained unfinished in Stuart's studio for 16 years (for Stuart characteristically refused to finish life portraits of his more distinguished subjects so they could be retained as sources for the numerous replicas which he produced for ready sale), and from the unquestionable visual evidence of the likeness itself. Kimball's ordering of the Stuart likenesses and the overwhelming objective evidence, of which the unbroken provenance tracing the portrait to Monticello is alone conclusive, establish beyond question the correctness of the identification of the Edgehill panel as Stuart's life portrait. It would be unnecessary to emphasize this were it not for the fact that a contrary claim was advanced by Orland and Courtney Campbell—that a canvas purchased at public auction in 1937, with no known history prior to that year, bearing a portrait that is manifestly the work of a hand decidedly inferior to Stuart, is the source of the Edgehill panel—a claim that must be rejected.

CHRONOLOGY: Jefferson himself stated that it was "soon after" the completion of this portrait that Stuart painted the medallion profile. With the completion of the latter dated with exactness to 7 June 1805, it is clear that the sitting for the Edgehill portrait took place shortly before this date, most probably at Stuart's studio at F and Seventh Streets in Washington. As he portrayed Jefferson at 62 for this portrait, Stuart was 49 and, as a friend told Dolley Madison, "all the rage."

HISTORY: Despite persistent attempts by Jefferson to obtain possession of this portrait, it was not until sixteen years after the sitting that he finally acquired it. In the meantime it remained unfinished in Stuart's studio, being used by him as the prototype for the various replicas. Henry Dearborn finally procured it from the painter and shipped it to Monticello where it arrived in August of 1821. It was there that the portrait hung for the remainder of Jefferson's life, descending, after his death, to the hands of his family at Edgehill where it hung for seventy-five years. In 1902 it was purchased by a collateral descendant of Jefferson, Burton Harrison, who took the painting to his residence in Scotland. The Babcock Galleries of New York purchased the panel from Harrison in 1927 for John B. Winant, who sold it to Percy S. Straus, from whom it passed by inheritance to Mr. Donald B. Straus of New York City. Its present joint-owners

18. The "Edgehill" portrait of Jefferson, painted from life by Gilbert Stuart in Washington shortly before the 7th of June 1805. The Thomas Jefferson Memorial Foundation and the National Portrait Gallery.

purchased it from Mr. Straus in 1983 with an agreement that the painting would be exhibited alternately at Monticello and the National Portrait Gallery.

PRESENT CONDITION: While the portrait was in his possession, Burton Harrison recorded that the panel had split "down the face," and reproductions made from it shortly after it left his hands show the likeness against a dark ground. Subsequently this dark ground and a considerable amount of repainting has been removed to reveal the delicate, transparently painted surface of the original.

ICONOGRAPHIC IMPORTANCE: It was late in Jefferson's second term that prints of this likeness, such as the handsome one by Robert Field, began displacing the prints of the 1800 Rembrandt Peale image in the public's popularity. The likeness was persistently reproduced in America and in France during Jefferson's later life, and after his death—especially after the Stuart likeness was adopted by the government as the official image of Jefferson for use on postage stamps and currency—it triumphed over the Peale to become unquestionably the preeminent icon of Jefferson.

COPIES: Only four replicas of this portrait are recorded. The earliest, painted for James Bowdoin between 1805 and 1807, survives in the Bowdoin College Museum of Fine Arts. What is undoubtedly the second of these replicas—that in the possession of James Madison in 1814—now hangs in the Governor's Palace at Colonial Williamsburg (a differing view is argued by David Meschutt). Two further replicas, one commissioned by John Doggett and one by George Gibbs, were painted as part of sets of the first five presidents and thus were created sometime after Monroe's election in 1816. The Doggett replica, destroyed in the 1851 Library of Congress fire, is known only through Maurin's 1825 lithograph and its derivatives. The Gibbs replica was sold by Colonel Gibbs's widow to Jefferson's great grandson, Thomas Jefferson Coolidge, whose descendants still own it. While the Gibbs replica seems seldom to have been reproduced, the destroyed Doggett image has been more frequently copied than perhaps any other of Jefferson's portraits. It was this version of Stuart's 1805 bust-size image that was chosen in 1867 to represent Jefferson officially on United States stamps, currency and certificates. At least fourscore of paintings and prints were derived from the Edgehill panel in the nineteenth century. Some thirty copies have been counted of the Bowdoin replica—many of them derived from Robert Field's 1807 engraving, which first set Stuart's portrait before the public. Less than a dozen copies of the Madison replica are known. Matthew Harris Jouett's copy of 1816, perhaps the first of the many painted from Stuart's 1805 *Jefferson,* was itself duplicated with some frequency.

REFERENCES: Bowen, 1892, 483–485; Hart, 1898, 54; Kimball, 1944, 512–523; Fiske Kimball, "Gilbert Stuart's Portraits of Jefferson," *Gazette des Beaux-Arts,* 6th Series, Vol. 26 (1944), 95-112; Orland and Courtney Campbell, *The Lost Portraits of Thomas Jefferson,* Amherst College, 1959; Adams, 1976, 305; Bush, 1976, 73–76; Cunningham, 1981, 1–2, 87–88, 90, 115, 141; David Meschutt, "Gilbert Stuart's Portraits of Thomas Jefferson," *The American Art Journal,* Volume XIII, Number 1, Winter 1981, 2–16.

19. The "medallion profile" of Jefferson, painted from life in June of 1805 in Washington by Gilbert Stuart. The Fogg Art Museum, Harvard University.

19. THE MEDALLION PROFILE BY GILBERT STUART

The Fogg Art Museum, Harvard University

MEDIUM: Kimball, believing the medium of this portrait to be oil on canvas, regarded as "careless allusions" Jefferson's description of it as "a profile in the medallion stile" executed in "water colours" and, at a later date, as a "sketch of me in the medallion form . . . on paper with crayons. . . ." But in 1956 Orland Campbell, after a careful examination of the original of this likeness, correctly concluded that both of Jefferson's descriptions, though seemingly in conflict, are actually accurate: that the portrait was executed in gouache—opaque watercolor—over a lightly indicated crayon drawing on handmade laid paper. The paper is mounted on thin linen, which in turn is mounted on modern artist's canvas and varnished, making the illusion that it was painted in oil almost complete except for the chain marks on the paper.

AUTHORSHIP: Jefferson not only recorded his payment to "Gilbert Stewart for drawing" this unsigned portrait, but little more than a week later sent him "his compliments" and a gift "for the trouble he gave him in taking the head á la antique." In 1813 Jefferson explained that of the three life portraits painted of him by Stuart the "third [was] in water colors, a profile in the medallion stile." Again, in 1819, Jefferson identified the author of this likeness by reporting that he had commissioned Stuart in 1805 "to sketch [him] in the medallion form." Thus both Stuart's authorship of the medallion profile and its place among the life portraits are amply recorded.

CHRONOLOGY: Jefferson undoubtedly sat for this portrait while he was "at the painting room of Mr. Stewart (the celebrated portrait painter) . . ." on the afternoon of the 7th of June 1805, for on that day he recorded his payment of one hundred dollars to Stuart "for drawing" his portrait. That this payment refers to the medallion portrait is confirmed not only by the letter that followed it on the 18th of June thanking Stuart again for "taking the head á la antique," but also by Jefferson's later explanation that the payment, "probably the treble of what he would have asked," was given to Stuart for ". . . the sketch . . . in the medallion form." Stuart was some thirteen years younger than the 62-year-old president when he sat for him in Stuart's studio at F and Seventh Streets in Washington.

HISTORY: The portrait was still in the hands of the painter on the 18th of June 1805 when Jefferson wrote that Stuart was "free to use either" the portrait in oils executed shortly before the medallion profile or the latter itself for the engravings that Stuart had contemplated having made from one of them. "The one not proposed to be used I will be glad to receive at Mr. Stewart's convenience; the other when he shall be done with it." Stuart chose to keep the earlier portrait for engraving and must have transmitted the medallion profile to Jefferson shortly before leaving Washington at the end of June. The portrait hung in the president's residence for the remaining years of Jefferson's presidency, leaving, with Jefferson in 1809, to become part of the collections at Monticello. Jefferson wrote of it in 1813 as being there in his possession, and two years later he generously lent the portrait to William Thornton in Washington for copying, though it was not returned until the Madisons brought it south with them after the inauguration of Madison's successor, some twenty-seven months after it had left Jefferson's hands. Two years after Jefferson's death the portrait was part of the exhibition of Jefferson's collection in Boston. After the dispersal of this collection through the Athenaeum sale, from which the medallion profile was reserved, it passed ultimately into the possession of the descendants of Jefferson's granddaughter, Ellen Wayles Randolph Coolidge, descending to the widow of Thomas Jefferson Newbold, who presented it in 1960 to the Fogg Art Museum in her husband's memory.

CONDITION: Long before its gift to Harvard University the surface of the painting had been lightly cleaned so that only traces of a yellowed varnish were still visible. Other than small areas, some of them retouched, where the paper has been rubbed through to the glue sizing beneath, the portrait is in good condition.

ICONOGRAPHIC IMPORTANCE: This is not only the portrait that Jefferson listed, with only the other likenesses by Stuart, in his reply to Delaplaine's request in 1813 to know the "approved portrait" of him, but was also that which Jefferson spoke of to Horatio Gates Spafford in February of 1815 as that "deemed the best which has been taken of me." Jefferson's own admiration for the likeness, as indicated in these statements and in his willingness to have it reproduced, seems to have been shared by his family. Martha Jefferson Randolph is said to have considered this the best of the two Stuart likenesses of her father that hung at Monticello and as "the portrait . . . which best gives the shape of his magnificent head and its peculiar pose." After Jefferson's death the husband of one of Jefferson's granddaughters wanted to "buy it . . . *at any price*" and in 1871 when Jefferson's great granddaughter, Sarah N. Randolph, compiled her "Domestic Life" of Jefferson, it bore the medallion profile as its frontispiece. Other of Jefferson's contemporaries agreed that it was a superior portrait. William Thornton, in fact, thought it "one of the finest [he] ever saw." William Birch pronounced it "the best thing that ever was done of" Jefferson, and the Duke of Saxe Weimar concluded that of the "several portraits of Mr. Jefferson" at Monticello "the best was that in profile by Stuart." It was, then, the portrait most admired by Jefferson, by his family, and by many of his most discriminating contemporaries.

COPIES: The earliest copy of the profile seems to have been that completed "about October 1805" by William Russell Birch, who saw the portrait in the president's Washington residence, borrowed it for two days, and made the drawing of it that he put into the hands of David Edwin as the source of Edwin's superb stipple engraving of 1809. From his own drawing, Birch again reproduced the medallion profile, this time as the "enamel portrait," which was exhibited in the "First Annual Exhibition of The Society of Artists of the United States" in Philadelphia in 1811. William Thornton's earliest copy of the profile was that "in Swiss crayons," which he placed in the Library of

62

Congress in 1816. At least two further versions of this profile were painted by Thornton, though, like almost all of these derivative likenesses, they are now unlocated. One of them may be that exhibited in the Diplomatic Reception Rooms of the Department of State, which Clement Conger believes to be by Thornton. Other notable copies were painted by Charles Bird King (now owned by Gordon Trist Burke) and Asher B. Durand. And although Thornton's original intention "to attempt to model [the medallion profile] in fine washed clay" seems never to have been carried out, Hiram Powers, much later in the century, did use the medallion portrait as the basis of the head of his full-length marble now in the House Wing of the Capitol at Washington.

REFERENCES: Bowen, 1892, 485; Hart, 1898, 48; Kimball, 1944, 512–523; George C. Mason, *Life and Works of Gilbert Stuart,* New York, 1879; Lawrence Park, *Gilbert Stuart,* New York, 1926, I, 439–443; Bernhard, Duke of Saxe-Weimar-Eisenach, *Travels through North America, During the Years 1825 and 1826,* Philadelphia, 1828, I, 199; report of 16 December 1956 from Orland Campbell to James A. Bear, Jr.; Bush, 1976, 76–80; Cunningham, 1981, 87–88, 92–93; David Meschutt, "Gilbert Stuart's Portraits of Thomas Jefferson," *The American Art Journal,* Volume XIII, Number 1, Winter 1981, 2–16.

20. The life portrait of Jefferson by Bass Otis, painted during the first week of June 1816 at Monticello. The Thomas Jefferson Memorial Foundation.

20. THE PORTRAIT BY BASS OTIS

The Thomas Jefferson Memorial Foundation

MEDIUM: Painted in oil on canvas, the portrait measures 30 x 25 inches.

AUTHORSHIP: The painting was commissioned by Joseph Delaplaine "for the express purpose" of serving as the source of the engraving published in his *Repository of the Lives and Portraits of Distinguished American Characters* in 1817. Advertisements announcing this publication and the inscription on the Jefferson print included in it ascribe the original likeness to Bass Otis. Documents among Jefferson's papers that record Otis's presence at Monticello not only confirm his authorship of this likeness but also establish it as a portrait painted from life. Since the painting mentioned by both Bowen and Hart as the original of this likeness has all the earmarks of a copy, Kimball, though he did not "determine whether any one" of the surviving versions of this likeness "is actually a life portrait," chose the painting now at Monticello to represent this image in his study of the life portraits. Stylistically this painting is manifestly the work of Otis, and the reverse of the portrait bears his studio label and his daughter's 1864 certification that the portrait "was Painted from Life by [her] Father Bass Otis . . . in 1816." But while this canvas is indisputably the work of Bass Otis, there has been doubt that it is the life portrait, and thus the source of Neagle's 1817 engraving, because of the obvious differences in the costumes of the two delineations and especially because the latter, unlike the bust-size painting, portrays Jefferson at half length with his hands folded in his lap. But the smaller size, the immediacy of the painting, and the summary treatment of the costume in the Monticello canvas are all attributes to be expected in the original of the portrait painted in the brief sittings at Monticello. The variations between this painting and the Neagle engraving may easily be the result of liberties taken by the engraver at the suggestion of Delaplaine to produce a print more in keeping with the other portraits published in the *Repository* series. Though Delaplaine claimed in his prospectus that a number of the portraits in his series would be engraved from portraits procured from life "at his own expense," others would be taken "from pictures already in possession of private families or public institutions." Since it was, then, the prints that were Delaplaine's objective and not the accumulation of a gallery of original paintings, and since he was financially unable to afford the cost of life portraits at times (he wrote Jefferson in February of 1816 that he could not afford to send an artist to paint his portrait), it is plausible that the life portrait should have been returned to Otis after the completion of Neagle's engraving, as partial payment for the painter's part in producing the image for reproduction in Delaplaine's engraved gallery of portraits. Thus the subsequent possession of the painting by Otis, rather than by Delaplaine, for whom it was expressly painted, supports the statement of the artist's daughter that this is the portrait "Painted from life by . . . Bass Otis . . . in 1816."

CHRONOLOGY: On 11 May 1816 Delaplaine announced to Jefferson that he had "engaged one of our best portrait painters, Mr. Otis of this City . . . to set out for your Mansion on the First day of June next, for the express purpose of painting your portrait for my work." Both publisher and painter arrived at Monticello on June 3rd, 1816—Otis carrying with him a letter of introduction from Dr. Caspar Wistar recommending him as "an artist of rising Character" distinguished "by his ingenuity as well as his obliging disposition." The portrait was completed shortly after their arrival, for Otis and Delaplaine's stay at Monticello was a brief one. Portraying Jefferson at 73, the artist was 31 years old at the time of the painting.

HISTORY: Immediately after its completion, the painting was carried by Otis and Delaplaine to Philadelphia where it was seen by William Thornton late in July of 1816. By October of the same year the canvas was in the hands of John Neagle, who was already at work on the engraving that Delaplaine issued early in 1817. In May of the following year it was part of the seventh annual exhibition at the Pennsylvania Academy of The Fine Arts and remained there for the Academy's subsequent exhibition in July. Apparently remaining in the artist's possession until his death in 1861, it passed into the hands of his daughter, Susan Otis. In 1864 it was transferred by her to John C. Trautwine whose granddaughter, Mrs. E. M. Bolles, presented the portrait in 1930 to the Thomas Jefferson Memorial Foundation. It has hung at Monticello since that date.

CONDITION: Cleaned and relined in 1959, the portrait survives in excellent condition.

ICONOGRAPHIC IMPORTANCE: After seeing Otis's portrait, William Thornton declared that "Never was such injustice done to [Jefferson] except by sign painters and General Kosciusko. . . ." Yet Neagle's engraving of 1817 was only the first of many prints which, judging from their popularity, brought this likeness to an extensive public that viewed Otis's image more charitably. Before the middle of the nineteenth century, prints of this portrait had been published not only in Philadelphia, New York and Boston but also in London and Glasgow, and when Peter Maverick's engraved version of the likeness was adopted as the official cypher of the Jefferson Insurance Company, the portrait was perpetuated endlessly on the company's official papers, making it the most widely distributed image of Jefferson in retirement.

COPIES: John Neagle's engraving, which faces page 125 in [Joseph] *Delaplaine's Repository of the Lives and Portraits of Distinguished American Characters*, Philadelphia, 1817, seems to have been the source of all subsequent prints of this likeness. It was also most probably the source of the four paintings now owned respectively by David K. E. Bruce, Miss Elizabeth L. Godwin, the University of Virginia, and the Yale University Art Gallery. Two further paintings, both derived ultimately from the Otis portrait and now unlocated, were at various times offered as portraits of Jefferson by Charles Willson Peale and Gilbert Stuart. A more notable copy of the original painting, perhaps a replica, once owned by William J. Campbell, was presented to the Chicago Historical Society in 1923 by the Iriquois Club.

REFERENCES: Bowen, 1892, 487; Hart, 1898, 48; Kimball, 1944, 525–7; Joseph Jackson, "Bass Otis, America's First Lithographer," *The Pennsylvania Magazine of History and Biography*, Vol. XXXVII, No. 4 (1913), 385–394; Caspar Wistar to Jefferson, 28 May 1816 in the Pierpont Morgan Library; the Jefferson-Delaplaine correspondence in the Jefferson Papers in the Library of Congress; Bush, 1976, 80–83.

21. The wax bas-relief of Jefferson sculpted from
life at Monticello shortly before 19 September 1816
by Giuseppe Valaperta. The New-York Historical
Society.

21. THE PORTRAIT BY GIUSEPPE VALAPERTA

The New-York Historical Society

MEDIUM: Valaperta's portrait was modeled directly in the surviving medium: a red wax bas-relief on black glass measuring 3 x 2 inches.

AUTHORSHIP: The bas-relief bears no inscription, but its provenance in the context of a collection of four other wax profiles, each of which it matches exactly in medium, size and style, and one of which bears Valaperta's signature, establishes this Italian medalist and sculptor as its author. Previous students have doubted that this portrait was modeled from life, but Valaperta's letter of introduction, endorsed by Jefferson on 16 September 1816, and the testimony of the Baron de Montlezun, who was at Montpelier when Valaperta returned from Monticello with the portrait, make its position among Jefferson's life portraits unquestionable.

CHRONOLOGY: Jefferson received Valaperta at Monticello on 16 September 1816 and sat for him either that day or shortly thereafter, for the sculptor arrived at Montpelier on the 19th with his wax profile of Jefferson. At Madison's residence, according to the Baron de Montlezun, Valaperta put the finishing touches to the Jefferson bas-relief with the hope of working it "afterwards in ivory." This wax portrait was produced during the Italian emigrant's first year in America and in an interlude from his employment sculpting ornaments for the National Capitol. Six months after modeling this depiction of Jefferson at 73 years of age, Valaperta disappeared from his Washington residence, presumably a suicide.

HISTORY: With seven other profiles of eminent Americans, the Jefferson wax portrait was purchased from Valaperta's estate by his executor after the sculptor's disappearance. Passing ultimately into the hands of the Gallatin family, it was presented to the New-York Historical Society in 1880.

CONDITION: Despite the fragile nature of the medium, this profile survives in good condition.

ICONOGRAPHIC IMPORTANCE: Although rarely seen and with virtually no influence in shaping the public image of Jefferson, this bas-relief is part of a series of wax portraits said to be faithful likenesses by the subjects' contemporaries.

COPIES: The ivory profile that Valaperta hoped to execute from the life portrait seems never to have been completed, and no portraits are known that have been derived from this wax profile.

REFERENCES: Kimball, 1944, 498; John Payne Todd to Jefferson, 14 September 1816, in the Jefferson Papers at the Massachusetts Historical Society; Baron de Montlezun, *Voyage fait dans les années 1816 et 1817 . . .*, Paris, 1818, I, 71–2; A. J. Wall, "Joseph Valaperta, Sculptor," *New-York Historical Society Quarterly Bulletin*, Vol. XI, No. 2 (July

1927), 53–6; Charles Fairman, *Art and Artists of the Capitol of the United States of America*, Washington, D.C., 1927, 452, 31, 32; *Catalogue of American Portraits in The New-York Historical Society*, New York, 1941, 160; Ethel Stanwood Bolton, *American Wax Portraits*, Boston, 1929, 30–31, 61; Bush, 1976, 83–85.

22. THE PORTRAIT BY
WILLIAM JOHN COFFEE

Unlocated

MEDIUM: "About half the size of life in plaster," this lost bust of Jefferson, if it were characteristic of other work executed by Coffee while at Monticello, would logically have been sculpted with the same delicacy of detail and diminutive scale as the artist's early work in porcelain.

AUTHORSHIP: In the postscript of his letter to John Adams of 17 May 1818, Jefferson wrote that "there is now here a Mr. Coffee, a sculptor and Englishman, who has just taken my bust. . . . He is a fine artist. He takes them about half the size of life in plaster." This statement and Jefferson's assurance to Madison that Coffee "gives less trouble than any artist, painter or Sculptor I have ever submitted myself to," establishes Coffee's authorship of a plaster bust of Jefferson sculpted from life. Though this portrait has apparently been lost since the dispersal of the Monticello collections, at least one extant plaster, that owned by Miss Olivia Taylor, has been erroneously identified as the Coffee likeness. This attribution, announced in 1945 by Anna Wells Rutledge, is now known to be an error not only because the Taylor plaster qualifies so consistently as one derived from the portrait by Peter Cardelli (see the following portrait) but also because the size, the undraped shoulders (Coffee's busts are invariably costumed), the scale of its detail, and the character of the modeling itself are all foreign to extant work unquestionably identified as that of Coffee.

CHRONOLOGY: The Coffee bust was completed while the artist was in his mid-forties either immediately before or on 11 April 1818—the day that Jefferson introduced the sculptor by letter to Madison as an artist "lately from England" who had come "from Richmond to take your bust and mine." While Coffee may again have been at Monticello on May 7th, when Jefferson, after an absence at Poplar Forest for more than a fortnight, wrote Adams that "Mr. Coffee . . . has just taken my bust," Jefferson's payment to this sculptor on the 12th of April "for the originals of 3. busts to wit Mrs. Randolph's Ellen's and mine" affirms that Jefferson's reference in this letter is to the completion of the bust on the earlier date, modeled one or two days before his 75th birthday.

HISTORY: Though busts by this artist of other members of the Monticello family have survived, nothing is known of the history of the Coffee *Jefferson* later than its completion in April of 1818.

CONDITION: It is possible that the original plaster or replicas in terra cotta of this portrait may yet survive, unidentified, in private or public collections.

ICONOGRAPHIC IMPORTANCE: Jefferson felt that Coffee was "really able in his art" and recommended him to Adams as "a fine artist." Extant portraits by Coffee indicate that Jefferson's recommendations were based on more than politeness and that Coffee's

71

Jefferson was an attractive and engaging likeness. That its influence was limited is evident from the silence that surrounds the history of this bust. It seems unlikely that it was ever known widely outside the family circle at Monticello.

COPIES: John S. Cogdell's report, in a letter to Samuel F. B. Morse in 1821, that Coffee had promised "a head of Mr. Jefferson at the North which he would send to me for the Society [The South Carolina Academy of Fine Arts]" indicates that the sculptor still had a duplicate of his *Jefferson* three years after its execution, but it is not known whether his promise to send the portrait to Charleston was kept. Perhaps, like his "strong wish to Model on [his] own Account, a Statue whole Length two feet 6 inches High, of Mr. Jefferson" in 1825, nothing further came of it.

REFERENCES: Hart, 1898, 47–48; Kimball, 1944, 532; Anna Wells Rutledge, "William John Coffee as a Portrait Painter," *Gazette des Beaux-Arts*, 6th series, Vol. XXVIII (Nov. 1945), [297]–312; George C. Groce, "William John Coffee, Long-lost Sculptor," *American Collector*, XV (May 1946), 14–15, 19–20; The Coffee-Jefferson correspondence in the Jefferson Papers at the Library of Congress; photographs of signed portrait busts by Coffee now in the Derby Museum and Art Gallery, England; Bush, 1976, 85–88.

The bust of Cornelia Jefferson Randolph by William John Coffee, sculptor of the lost portrait of Jefferson executed from life in May of 1818 at Monticello. The Thomas Jefferson Memorial Foundation.

23. THE PORTRAIT BY PETER CARDELLI

Destroyed

MEDIUM: A helpful description of the process used by Cardelli to produce his portrait busts is that recorded in John Quincy Adams's diary: "The first mould is taken in soft red clay worked by the hand, the second is [a] Plaister Shell moulded over it in two halves. The Bust itself is cast in this. . . ." It was this cast that Cardelli called "the plaster original." Thus the destroyed life portrait was of the same substance as its surviving copies.

AUTHORSHIP: The original plaster may have been signed, as is the sculptor's extant bust of Trumbull, below the right shoulder: "P. Cardelli F." Though the original of this bust survived into the twentieth century, the Cardelli likeness is among the last of Jefferson's portraits to be correctly identified. When the original left Edgehill at the turn of the century, its authorship was unknown. And though Hart and Kimball were aware of the correspondence that affirms Cardelli's execution of a portrait of Jefferson sculpted from life, only Kimball attempted to identify it, though he confused the Edgehill plaster with still another bust of Jefferson—one now identified as a copy of the posthumous portrait by Sidney Morse. When, in 1945, one of the casts of the destroyed Edgehill bust was finally attributed to an artist, the identification was a mistaken one: William John Coffee (see entry under his name in this catalogue). That the plasters derived from the Edgehill bust are copies of the original portrait sculpted by Cardelli at Monticello is now established by the consistently positive results of the comparison of these busts with portraits unquestionably by Cardelli, which they match in size, in medium, in stylistic conception, in technique of execution, and even in such details as the absence of drapery and the squarely cut form of the base. There has often been confusion as to whether the first name of the Cardelli who sculptured Jefferson was Georgio or Pietro, but the artist's broadside subscription forms for copies of this bust appeared under the name of "Peter Cardelli."

CHRONOLOGY: John Quincy Adams urged Jefferson to grant Cardelli a sitting, and when Jefferson agreed to welcome the sculptor to Monticello for the purpose, Adams provided a further letter of introduction. This letter, which Cardelli carried with him, was endorsed on 24 May 1819—the day of Cardelli's arrival at Monticello. The bust, then, must have been modeled shortly after that date when Jefferson was 76 years of age. Cardelli's age is unknown, but Jefferson's sitting was only one of a series of sculpturing opportunities—including sittings with Monroe, Adams and Madison— which fell to the sculptor that year and induced him to leave his employment carving ornaments on the Capitol in the optimistic hope that he could support himself by the sale of plaster casts of his busts of eminent Americans.

HISTORY: Cardelli left not only a plaster bust for Jefferson at Monticello but also either the mold from which it was produced or yet another plaster cast of it, and perhaps

73

23. A twentieth-century plaster cast of the original plaster bust (now destroyed) of Jefferson modeled from life at Monticello on the 24th of May 1819 by Peter Cardelli. The Thomas Jefferson Memorial Foundation.

other busts as well. Low water delayed the shipment of these materials until late that year when, with the exception of the original plaster, they were returned to the artist's possession. After the sale of Monticello in 1830 the bust was moved to Edgehill, where it eventually became part of the property of Carolina Ramsay Randolph, the sole owner of Edgehill at the time of her death in 1902. When, at that time, the Edgehill relics from Monticello were left to three of her nieces, the Cardelli bust came into the possession of one of them, Cornelia Jefferson Taylor. Because of a broken pedestal, this plaster had apparently been stored in the Edgehill attic for some time. The bust subsequently was at Lego, the residence of Cornelia Jefferson Taylor, for several years. Sometime after its acquisition from Edgehill in 1903 and before 1910 a concern in New York City was engaged to produce plaster reproductions of this bust. In the process of executing these casts, the original is said to have been destroyed.

ICONOGRAPHIC IMPORTANCE: The influence of the Cardelli bust in the nineteenth century was slight. Apparently Cardelli's plans for subscription were not successful, and his portrait of Jefferson was neither duplicated as frequently nor distributed as widely as the artist hoped. Though Cardelli often had difficulty in producing satisfactory representations of his subjects (John Quincy Adams, during a series of sittings, felt that Cardelli would "ultimately not get a likeness"), this bust is recognizably Jefferson.

CONDITION: The original plaster is said to have been destroyed sometime between 1903 and 1910 in the process of making a cast for reproducing the bust for commercial sale. The copies of this bust, in plaster like the original, survive in good condition.

COPIES: No examples of this likeness that might have been cast as replicas and sold to subscribers in response to Cardelli's broadside have been located. The number of casts taken from the original plaster by the New York firm that reproduced it before 1910 is not known, but at least four of these survive. One is owned by the Thomas Jefferson Memorial Foundation; another by Margaret Randolph Taylor and Olivia Taylor of Charlottesville. The example at Redlands, Albemarle County, is owned by Robert Carter. Another example was owned by the late Mary Walker Randolph.

REFERENCES: Hart, 1898, 47; Kimball, 1944, 498; *Catalogue of Portraits and Other Works of Art in the Possession of The American Philosophical Society*, Philadelphia, 1961, 1–2; Charles E. Fairman, *Art and Artists of the Capitol of the United States of America*, Washington, 1927, 46; the Cardelli correspondence at the Massachusetts Historical Society; the Cardelli-Trumbull correspondence at the Morristown National Historical Park; report of Miss Olivia Taylor; the Cardelli broadside in the Madison Papers at the Library of Congress; Bush, 1976, 88–91.

24. The life portrait of Jefferson painted by Thomas Sully at Monticello in March of 1821. The American Philosophical Society.

24. THE PORTRAIT BY THOMAS SULLY

The American Philosophical Society

MEDIUM: Painted in oil on canvas, the portrait measures 30 x 25 inches.

AUTHORSHIP: The public nature of this commission and the fame of the likeness that resulted from it are such that Sully's authorship of this portrait has been continually acknowledged. The artist's monogram and his notation that this portrait was painted "From Jefferson, 1821; finished 1830"—both inscribed on the reverse of the canvas at the American Philosophical Society—distinguish this half-length from its replicas as the portrait painted from life.

CHRONOLOGY: Late in January of 1821 Jefferson was informed of the desire of the "Superintendent, Officers, Professors, Instructors, and Cadets of the U. States Mil. Academy" to commission Thomas Sully to paint a portrait of him to be added to those hanging in the "Academic Library" as "being alike one of the Founders, and Patrons of both" "Our Republic . . . and the Mil. Academy." Jefferson responded cordially and though he felt that the trouble of Sully's journey would be "illy bestowed on an ottamy of 78," he nevertheless agreed to the sitting, which took place at Monticello in March of 1821. According to Dunlap the 37-year-old Sully "was an inmate of Monticello twelve days, and left the place with the greatest reluctance."

HISTORY: In 1830 on the commission of William Short, who presented the portrait to the American Philosophical Society in June of that year, the artist added the finishing touches to the portrait that Jefferson had posed for nine years earlier. The painting has hung for over a century and a half in an honored position in Philosophical Hall in Philadelphia, home of the distinguished institution over which Jefferson presided as president from 1797 until 1814.

CONDITION: Soundly painted and free of the repainting of later "restorers," the portrait survives in excellent condition. A modern relining has covered the original inscription on the reverse of the painting.

ICONOGRAPHIC IMPORTANCE: As its frequent reproduction bears testimony, Sully's portrait offers us the finest image of the Jefferson of the late Monticello years. Surviving in untampered condition the portrait is an unusually reliable record of Jefferson's coloring, depicting accurately the fresh complexion and the traces of the sandy hue still in his hair and eyebrows. Not only has the life portrait moved the participants of the distinguished conclaves that gather annually in Philosophical Hall, but its extensive reproductions, in replicas, copies, engravings, and transmutations into sculpture, have given the Sully likeness a far-reaching and admiring audience. As the ultimate source of the great full-length at West Point, the portrait is also significant as one of but two portrayals of Jefferson at full length, for his imposing stature was a memorable aspect of his presence. There is no better testimony of the effect of the West Point image on its viewers than that of James Fenimore Cooper. At West Point in April of 1823 Cooper, whose "antipathies . . . to Mr. Jefferson" were well known, was induced, despite the fact that he insisted that he would rather "have gone twice as far to see the picture of almost any other man," to enter the library to view Sully's recently installed full-length of Jefferson. On his first confrontation with the painting, Cooper "desired the gentlemen with [him] to wait, until [he] could go" for Mr. Charles Mathews, his guest, a distinguished British comedian and also "a collector, and . . . a very respectable critic." Mathews, wrote Cooper later, "pronounced it one of the finest portraits he had ever beheld, and that he would never have forgiven me if I had let it escape his notice. But you will smile when I tell you its effects on myself. There was a dignity, a repose, I will go further, and say a loveliness, about this painting, that I never have seen in any other portrait. . . . I saw . . . Jefferson, standing before me, not in red breeches and slovenly attire, but a gentleman, appearing in all republican simplicity, with a grace and ease on the canvas, that to me seem unrivalled. It has really shaken my opinion of Jefferson as a man, if not as a politician; and when his image occurs to me now, it is in the simple robes of Sully, sans red breeches, or even without any of the repulsive accompaniments of a political 'sans culotte.'"

COPIES: Recognizing that this life portrait was used as the prototype for the upper portion of both the small full-length completed by Sully on 10 April 1822 (now owned by Edward S. Moore) and the large full-length finished on the 7th of May of the same year (now hanging, as it did in Jefferson's time, at West Point), Kimball nevertheless suggested that the related full-length sketch by Sully owned by John Hill Morgan was a study painted from life rather than from the half-length. Another related sketch, brought to light since Kimball's study, and now owned by Hugh Murray Savage, has also been suggested as a life study. However, the fact that every detail of the pose and even the lighting in both of these watercolor sketches duplicates exactly what is found in the original half-length and that they possess the addition of ficticious settings can only lead to the conclusion that both were studies for the West Point full-length based on the half-length life portrait. While it seems likely that Sully, during his stay at Monticello, would have sketched Jefferson's full stature for the projected full-length, until such a sketch is found with earmarks that clearly distinguish it from the studies taken from the half-length, the suggestion that Sully sketched Jefferson from life at full length must remain an unsupported one. Among the many replicas of the original half-length, the most notable are the painting once owned by President Monroe, which is now in the possession of the Jefferson Society at the University of Virginia; that purchased by the federal government in 1874 which now hangs in the Senate Corridor of the United States Capitol; and a canvas, once in the possession of Lafayette, which is currently unlocated. The latter was used by David d'Angers in producing his bronze full-length of Jefferson, the head of which, according to Lossing, "was modeled chiefly from an excellent portrait by Sully, in the possession of LaFayette." The David d'Angers likeness, and thus the Sully, was again used by a sculptor when Moses Ezekiel produced his bust of Jefferson. J. W. Casilear included the Sully *Jefferson* in his engraved series of presidents in 1834 and thus produced the first of many prints of the Sully likeness.

REFERENCES: Bowen, 1892, 485–6; Hart, 1898, 55; Kimball, 1944, 527–31; Edward Biddle and Mantle Fielding, *The Life and Works of Thomas Sully*, Philadelphia, 1921, 191; James Franklin Beard (Ed.), *The Letters and Journals of James Fenimore Cooper*, Cambridge, 1960, I, 95–6; *A Catalogue of Portraits and Other Works of Art in the American Philosophical Society*, Philadelphia, 1961, 54–5; Adams, 1976, 96; Bush, 1976, 91–94; Joseph Vaughan and Omer Allen Gianniny, Jr., *Thomas Jefferson's Rotunda Restored, 1973–76*, Charlottesville, 1981, 150.

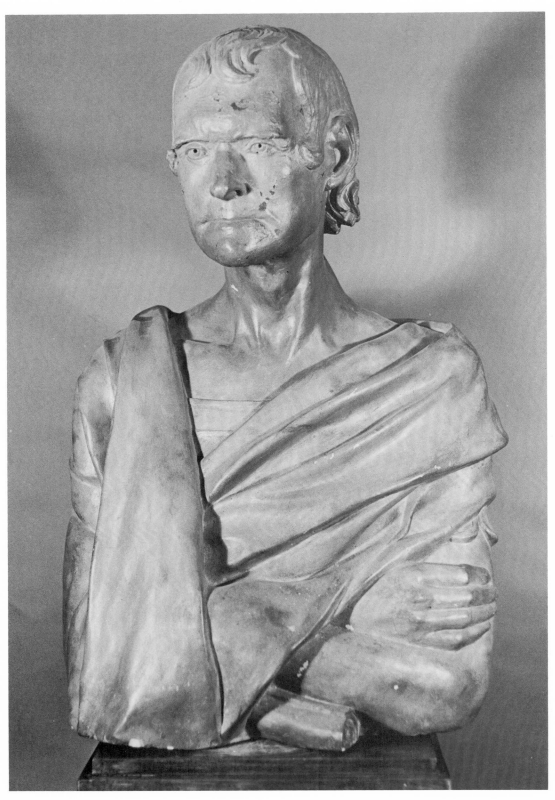

25. The original plaster cast from the life mask that was molded directly from the "living person" of Jefferson on the 15th of October 1825 at Monticello. New York State Historical Association, Cooperstown.

25. THE PORTRAIT BY
JOHN HENRI ISAAC BROWERE

New York State Historical Association, Cooperstown.

MEDIUM: The method and the exact nature of the medium used by Browere in casting his life masks were closely guarded secrets never transmitted beyond his son, Albertus. Jefferson was able to record only that the process involved "Successive coats of thin grout plaistered on the naked head, and kept there an hour." The liquid substance (Jefferson referred to it as such in the first draft of his description of the sitting) used by Browere for the cast was undoubtedly the same used so successfully in executing his other portraits, so it must have been conditions peculiar to the atmosphere at Monticello that allowed this liquid to dry so rapidly "that separation became difficult and even dangerous" and obliged Browere to "use freely the mallet and chisel to break it into pieces and get off a piece at a time." From this repaired mould of Jefferson's "living person," was cast, in plaster, the life portrait into which such details as the open eyes and the hair were cut directly by the artist.

AUTHORSHIP: Though unsigned, the very nature of this "life mask" and its provenance with the body of Browere's portraits have made its position among the life portraits and its authorship by Browere unquestionable.

CHRONOLOGY: In a nineteenth-century transcript of a certificate, dated 15 October 1825, which survives among Browere's papers, Jefferson certifies that "Mr. Browere has this day made a mould in Plaister composition, from my person for the purposes of making a portrait Bust and Statue for his contemplated National Gallery." The plaster cast from this mold into which Browere cut the open eyes, the hair and other details was almost certainly completed before the sculptor left Monticello, since Madison, on the 19th of October, certified that "a Bust . . . taken by Mr. Browere from the person of Mr. Jefferson, has been submitted to our inspection and appears to be a faithful Likeness."

HISTORY: Browere's work in collecting his gallery of life masks was monumental, but was unappreciated in his time and thus "on his death Bed he wished the Heads of the Principle ones to be detached, Boxed up and nothing done with them for 40 years." Complying with this request, his son, Albertus, closeted them until the centennial of the signing of the Declaration of Independence, when he set to work remounting the busts, "Putting Drapery to Some," hoping that they would be exhibited in Philadelphia during the centennial celebration and might ultimately be purchased by the government. But even in the interest in America's historic past that was generated by the centennial, neither the government nor the committee in charge of the centennial exhibitions seems to have shown interest in Browere's life masks, and they lapsed once again into obscurity. It was Charles Henry Hart who rediscovered them in 1897 still in the care of the artist's descendants and made them and their significance public knowledge. Fearing the dispersal of the collection, Hart, as had Albertus Browere before him, urged, unsuccessfully, that the government purchase it *en bloc*. Hart further suggested that the most important of the life masks be "cast in imperishable bronze." It was not until 1940, however, and then by a private individual, Stephen Clark, that the main body of the collection was purchased, duplicated in bronze and placed on permanent loan at the New York State Historical Association at Cooperstown. On Mr. Clark's death in 1960, the collection, including Browere's *Jefferson*, passed to the Association as a gift with the injunction that neither the original nor the bronze replica should ever leave Cooperstown.

CONDITION: Kimball stated that the bust of Jefferson had been "more than once repaired," but a careful examination of the original plaster reveals no detectable repairs. The whole plaster is covered with a putty-colored glossy finish, which most probably was applied when the busts were refurbished by Albertus Browere in 1876. This finish has flaked in a few places, but there is no evidence of any significant damage.

ICONOGRAPHIC IMPORTANCE: Madison was joined in his certification of the accuracy of Browere's likeness of Jefferson by contemporaries whose judgments of works of art were informed and candid. Samuel F. B. Morse found it a "perfect facsimile" and Rembrandt Peale, whose own two portraits of Jefferson record his penetrating knowledge of the subject's lineaments, thought Browere's portrayal "in truth a faithful and a living Likeness." It was, however, Browere's polychrome full-length version of this portrait, unveiled on the hour of Jefferson's death, which the artist said "gave an effect . . . which will not ever be forgotten . . . by the thousands" who viewed it in New York's City Hall during the celebrations of the semi-centennial of the Declaration of Independence. But Browere's report of the impact of his *Jefferson* upon his contemporaries is obviously exaggerated, as his own subsequent decision to retire it into obscurity indicates. It was not until its rediscovery at the end of the nineteenth century that it was recognized as "the most faithful portrait possible, down to the minutest detail, the very living features of the breathing man, a likeness of the greatest historical significance and importance."

COPIES: In May of 1826 Browere began work on a full-length portrayal of Jefferson, based on his life mask, which was to be presented, for the duration of the celebrations on the 4th of July of that year, to the Corporation of New York "to be publickly exhibited to all who desire to view the beloved features of the friend of science and of liberty." The sculptor wrote Jefferson on the 13th of June that on that day he had "completed your full-length statue (nudity) and to-morrow I intend, if spared, to commence dressing it in the costume you wore at the time of your delivery of the Declaration of American Independence." Though Jefferson was too ill to respond to Browere's request for "a full and explicit account of the form and colour of his dress," the artist was able after "unremitting exertions, to finish and place it in [the City Hall banqueting-room], exactly at the hour of the dissolution of Mr. Jefferson." There this full-length, colored and clothed statue represented Jefferson's "lofty and majestic figure standing erect; his mild blue and expressive eyes beaming with intelligence and good will to his fellow men.

82

The scroll of the Declaration . . . clutched in his extended right hand. . . . His left hand resting on the hip. . . ." No trace of this statue has been found nor of any portrait that might have resulted from Browere's offer to the University of Virginia to "erect in marble or bronze a statue to the memory of its founder." The only duplication of the Browere *Jefferson* now extant is the bronze replica cast on Mr. Clark's commission in 1940.

REFERENCES: Hart, 1898, 47; Kimball, 1944, 523–3; "Certificates Relative to the Busts of General LaFayette Executed in Plaister by John H. I. Browere" at the New York State Historical Association; James Madison to Jefferson, 14 June 1825 in the Madison Papers at the Library of Congress; the Browere-Jefferson correspondence in the Jefferson Papers at the Library of Congress; Charles Henry Hart, "Unknown Life Masks of Great Americans," *McClure's Magazine*, Vol. IX, No. 6 (Oct. 1897), 1053–60; Charles Henry Hart, *Browere's Life Masks of Great Americans*, New York, 1899; correspondence with Louis C. Jones; Bush, 1976, 95–98.

A pencil drawing of Jefferson attributed at various times to both Benjamin Latrobe and John Trumbull, now thought to be derived from the Houdon bust.

A NOTE ON FURTHER PORTRAITS

EXCLUDED from this catalogue are a number of portraits, both suppositional and existing, which have been put forward at various times as part of the canon of Jefferson's life likenesses. These include posthumous portraits, based on one or more of the identified life portraits, which clearly have no place among those likenesses created in Jefferson's presence, portraits of unidentified subjects erroneously identified as portrayals of Jefferson, and a number of rumored "portraits" whose existence has never been established. Only the most noteworthy of these are indicated briefly here.

LATROBE: The drawing attributed to Benjamin Latrobe in the 1962 exhibition of Jefferson's life portraits has become the focus, despite its enduring appeal, of increasing questions. Once editorial work on the Latrobe papers called into question Latrobe's authorship of the drawing, E. P. Richardson attributed it to John Trumbull ("A Life Drawing of Jefferson by John Trumbull," *The American Art Journal*, Volume VII, No. 2 [Nov. 1975]). But given the documentation of all other Trumbull portraits of Jefferson—replicas as well as the life portrait—it is difficult to believe that so beguiling a life-likeness could be created completely off the record. Jefferson's sense of his historical obligations when it came to portraits created in his presence—most particularly with someone of Trumbull's importance—is amply recorded in this catalogue. Once we accept that the authorship is problematic and that no documentation from Jefferson sheds light on its status as a life portrait, it is not difficult to suspect that this lively little drawing may well be derived not from life but from one of the greatest of Jefferson's life portraits—that by Houdon.

EPPINGTON: Eva Turner Clark, in her study of *Francis Epes, His Ancestors and Descendants* (New York, 1942, 253), quotes Egbert Giles Leigh, Jr. (1851–1915) as writing "It is a matter of real distress to me that so many of the Eppington portraits and old relics are lost. Among the portraits was one of Mr. and Mrs. Jefferson, presented by Mrs. Jefferson to Mr. and Mrs. Francis Eppes." Unfortunately further record of such a gift or even of the existence of this double portrait has not been found.

DU SIMITIÈRE: In 1959 Paul Sifton suggested as a portrait of Jefferson drawn about 1776, the miniature likeness in plumbago on ivory among the Du Simitière materials at the Historical Society of Pennsylvania (*Antiques*, Vol. LXXVI, No. 3 [Sept. 1959], 250–1). There are such significant differences between the features of the individual represented in this Du Simitière drawing and those of Jefferson as recorded in his established portraits, however, that the miniature cannot be accepted as a depiction of Jefferson. From a study of the costume of this miniature, Frederick P. Todd, Director of the Museum at West Point, concluded that the personage in the ivory "is definitely in a uniform" and that it is probably that "of an English junior officer of about the period of the American Revolution."

COSWAY: It has more than once been suggested that Maria Cosway depicted Jefferson during the many opportunities she had to observe him in Paris, but the absence of any record of such a portrait and the restriction of Mrs. Cosway's references concerning Jefferson likenesses to the Trumbull miniature—the only portrait of the American that she bequeathed with her other effects to the Collegio at Lodi—strongly suggest that this replica was the only depiction of Jefferson in her hands.

PARADISE: The inventory of 1812 of the Paradise house in Williamsburg mentions a large portrait of Jefferson, but whether it was part of the Paradise household in Europe, and thus most probably a replica of Mather Brown's canvas, or was acquired after the return to the United States, is unknown. It is most likely, though, that this portrait was derived from one of the likenesses described in this catalogue.

RAMAGE: The late Mrs. Breckinridge Long had in her possession at one time a miniature said to be a portrait of Jefferson by John Ramage (Frick Art Reference Library files). Until this portrait can again be located, it cannot be determined whether Jefferson actually sat to Ramage when both were in New York City during Jefferson's first months as secretary of state.